PLANET DINOSAUR

PLANET DINOSAUR

THE NEXT GENERATION OF GIANT KILLERS

CAVAN SCOTT

Palaeontology specialist
Dr Darren Naish

BBC
BOOKS

CONTENTS

INTRODUCTION

We are living in a golden age of dinosaur discoveries. Every year new fossil finds reveal brand new species of dinosaur and bring quantum leaps in our knowledge of how and where these legendary monsters lived and died.

The first dinosaurs evolved around 240–230 million years ago, during the middle of the Triassic period. But it wasn't until the beginning of the Jurassic period, about 40 million years later, that they became the dominant creatures on Earth, occupying the roles once played by other reptile groups. And there they stayed, reigning supreme, developing new ways to exploit their environment and new ways to kill, until (with the exception of their direct descendants, the birds) they were wiped out by an earth-shattering event, 65 million years ago.

In 1999, *Walking with Dinosaurs* first aired on the BBC and revolutionized the way we thought of dinosaurs, using a mixture of computer-generated imagery (CGI) and animatronics to bring the hulking monsters of prehistory to life. The dinosaurs' everyday lives were portrayed as if we were watching a natural history documentary, on safari millions of years ago. Twelve years on, *Planet Dinosaur* picks up the story. The CGI has moved on, but so has our understanding of life back in the Triassic, Jurassic and Cretaceous ages.

Planet Dinosaur, accompanied by this book, examines some of the most amazing dino-discoveries of the last three decades. From the lush forests of China and the wild heat of equatorial Africa, to the dusty plains of South America and the frozen wastes of the Arctic, we will come face to face with biological killing machines, titanic giants and bizarre, almost alien, beasts. We will meet terrifying sea monsters, wily hunters and vicious cannibals. And, finally, we will experience the cataclysmic disaster that wiped these seemingly unstoppable creatures from the face of the Earth.

Of course, there are still many secrets buried deep underground, and more discoveries yet to be made. And while there are still many things that we don't yet understand, these are exactly the sorts of issues that make palaeontology so exciting. Every new discovery opens up new possibilities and new ideas about how these spectacular creatures lived and died. As we'll see, some of the ideas involve extrapolation and clever lateral thinking: scientists often struggle to understand the world as it once was, when so many pieces of the puzzle are missing. Experts often have to make the best possible guesses using evidence provided by the remains of other dinosaur species and by what we know of animals living today. Palaeontologists don't always see eye to eye when it comes to the interpretation of the evidence, but they all share the same love of all things prehistoric.

They also all agree that Planet Dinosaur was a spectacular, if dangerous, place to live.

THE CHANGING FACE OF PLANET DINOSAUR

MIDDLE AND LATE TRIASSIC

When the first dinosaurs evolved about 240 million years ago, the world looked very different. All dry land was grouped together into the huge megacontinent Pangaea.

LATE JURASSIC

Fast forward about 80 million years and Pangaea has split into two immense land masses. The northern continent is called Laurasia and the southern one is Gondwana.

LATE CRETACEOUS

As we enter the Late Cretaceous epoch, the world is looking more like the one we know today. Both Laurasia and Gondwana have broken up into smaller continents, and North and South America are separated by water. Europe 94 million years ago existed as an archipelago: warm, shallow seas covered all the low-lying areas.

THE LATE JURASSIC WORLD   THE LATE CRETACEOUS WORLD

JURASSIC
JARGON BUSTING

Explaining some of the main types of creatures you'll discover in *Planet Dinosaur*:

SAURISCHIANS (Sore-IS-kee-anz)

One of the two main dinosaur groups. Their pelvic bones were arranged much like those of lizards, hence the name, which means 'lizard-hipped'. They shared proportionally long necks, a large thumb and other detailed features. Most kinds possessed air-filled bones.

ORNITHISCHIANS (Or-ni-THIS-kee-anz)

The other main dinosaur group alongside the saurischians. Their pelvic bones were arranged much like those of modern birds, hence the name 'bird-hipped', but they did not include the ancestors of birds (birds are actually saurischians).

OVIRAPTOROSAURS (OH-vi-RAP-tor-oh-sorz)

A group of bird-like, beaked theropods, some of which boasted colourful plumage. Advanced kinds had toothless jaws but were equipped with two tooth-like prongs on their palates.

PALAEONTOLOGISTS (Pal-e-on-TOL-o-gists)

An usually intelligent modern primate that studies the fossilized remains of plant and animals. Often found digging bones out of the ground in harsh conditions or holed up in museums and universities. They don't always agree with each other.

PTEROSAURS (TER-o-sores)

The earliest vertebrates known to have evolved true, powered flight. Long arms and finger bones supported membranous wings. Pterosaurs are often mistakenly identified as dinosaurs. This is incorrect, although the so-called 'winged lizards' were close relatives of dinosaurs.

SAUROPODS (Sore-o-podz)

A group of especially long-necked, plant-eating, quadrupedal saurischians. The group included some of the largest animals ever to have lived. Their name means 'lizard foot'.

THEROPODS (THAIR-o-podz)

With a name that means 'beast foot', these bipedal saurischian dinosaurs were largely predatory, though some were omnivores or herbivores. Wishbones and feathers evolved within this group. During the Jurassic the group of theropods called birds emerged: the only dinosaur group to survive beyond the end of the Cretaceous to the present day.

TYRANNOSAURIDS (Ti-RAN-o-SORE-idz)

The 'tyrant lizards' were the ultimate killers. Large-headed theropods with tiny arms, powerful hind legs and massive, powerful jaws lined with thickened, spike-like teeth. Tyrannosaurids belonged to a larger group termed the tyrannosauroids, the early members of which were small, feathered predators.

THE AGE OF THE DINOSAURS (see also *The Dinosaurs in Context*, pages 230–32):

227 ma	Late Triassic epoch
199 ma	Early Jurassic
175 ma	Middle Jurassic
161 ma	Late Jurassic
146 ma	Early Cretaceous
99 ma	Late Cretaceous

ma = million years ago

THE

It is only in recent years that the biggest dinosaurs that ever lived – the icons of Planet Dinosaur – have been unearthed. How and why did these titans grow so immense, and could any animal attack these new giants?

NEW GIANTS

A GIANT DISCOVERY

Cracks begin to splinter across the surface of the egg. It shakes ever so slightly as the tiny creature inside fights to get out, thrashing against the brittle shell. The cracks widen and shatter as the top of the egg is finally pushed away. The infant's slender neck unfurls as it breaks the sac of viscous liquid that has kept it alive so far.

The newly hatched dinosaur raises its head, feeling the warmth of the Cretaceous sun against its scales. Tentatively, it takes its first ever look at the outside world; squinting against the sudden, alien brightness. As it struggles to focus, to take in the desolate plains that stretch out under a brooding, stormy sky, it is cast in shadow. With a flap of leathery wings, death swoops down from the sky. The hatchling looks up, straight into the eyes of the chaoyangopterid pterosaur that has landed nearby, attracted to the myriad nests that dot the landscape. With a wingspan of over a metre, this aerial hunter is just as deadly on the ground as it was in the air.

The hatchling cries out in alarm as the toothless beak snaps towards the nest. It dodges the chaoyangopterid at first, but it won't evade it for long. Finally, the pterosaur manages to catch the hatchling in its beak, but the helpless infant is still slick with the fluid from within the egg and slips from the pterosaur's grip, tumbling back into the nest. The pterosaur's head bobs down again, but suddenly stops short. The ground is vibrating to the sound of heavy footsteps. Something large is heading their way. The chaoyangopterid's head snaps around to spy a large abelisaurid dinosaur running towards the nest site. The flying reptile takes to the air. While it's happy to feed on helpless hatchlings, taking on a full-grown, and probably quite angry, parent is something else...

WALKING ON EGGS

In 1997 a joint team of palaeontologists from the American Museum of Natural History in New York and the Carmen Funes Municipal Museum in Argentina were on the hunt for fossils in the heat of the Patagonian badlands. Not expecting to find anything spectacular, they stepped onto the mudstone flat, scouring the ground for telltale signs of fossils. Five minutes later they realized they had stumbled upon something big.

The team had discovered the biggest dinosaur nest site the world had ever seen. Dating back to the Late Cretaceous, between 70 to 90 million years ago, the site stretched out for 2.6 square kilometres (a square mile) in front of them and was so full of eggs that it was virtually impossible to take a step without crushing shell fragments beneath their feet. The amazed research team renamed the site *Auca Mahuevo*, after *huevos*, the Spanish for eggs.

Among the tens of thousands of eggs scattered across Auca Mahuevo, many were unhatched. Amazingly, some even contained the embryonic remains of sauropods that had died millions of years ago. Exquisitely detailed, some of the embryos even had fossilized skin still on the bones, and their articulated jaws, peg-shaped teeth and tiny nostrils were all well preserved, enabling them to be identified as members of the sauropod group, Titanosauria.

DEATH BEFORE LIFE

Why did so many embryos die without hatching? In Cretaceous times the badlands would have looked very different, with streams criss-crossing the plains that often flooded. It's thought that the eggs at Auca Mahuevo were victims of one of these floods. When the waters subsided, the eggs were buried beneath thick silt. The mud protected the eggs, both from the elements and also from scavengers such as the chaoyangopterid. The same cycle probably happened on and off for more than a million years, meaning that even more eggs might await discovery.

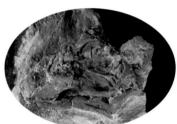

THE WORLD'S OLDEST DINOSAUR EMBRYOS

While the embryos at Auca Mahuevo were a staggering find, much older remains have been unearthed elsewhere. In 1976 fossil eggs were discovered in South Africa that dated back to the Early Jurassic, 190 million years ago, and contained skeletons of unhatched *Massospondylus*, a prosauropod that was an ancestor of the gargantuan sauropod. The remains are the oldest known embryos of any land-dwelling backboned animal.

The baby dinosaur screams out in terror as an abelisaurid tears towards it. The gigantic carnivore surveys the nest at its feet. Its nostrils flare as it drops its head to the hatchling. Almost tenderly the giant picks the quaking hatchling up by its tail, only to whip it back down against the ground, killing the defenceless creature instantly.

NEST RAIDER

If titanosaur eggs did survive, there was no guarantee that infants would make it past their first hour of life. Hatchling sites throughout the world were dangerous places for newborns, as our hatchling found out.

This is *Skorpiovenator*, a nest-raiding predator that scavenged for carrion and preyed on young dinosaurs. *Skorpiovenator* didn't hunt for scorpions. It was given its name because of the abundance of living scorpions that scuttled around the excavation site where it was found. The discovery of *Skorpiovenator* was particularly exciting as the skeleton was almost complete, lacking only the right forearm and the end half of its tail.

Its skull is short, stout and covered in ridges, furrows and tubercles – bumpy nodules that are scattered over the heads of most abelisaurid theropods. It has short, stubby, near-useless arms, but strong legs with powerful thighs and sturdy shins over which its 1.8-tonne (2-ton) body was balanced. Its slender jaws housed rows of razor-sharp teeth.

But *Skorpiovenator*, like all bullies, probably only picked on creatures its own size, or much, much smaller. It certainly wouldn't take on the baby's true parent –

one of the largest dinosaurs that has ever been found.

▶ *ARGENTINOSAURUS*

SKORPIOVENATOR
LOOMS OVER AN
ARGENTINOSAURUS
HATCHLING

WALKING WITH GIANTS

ARGENTINOSAURUS HUINCULENSIS

TRANSLATION
Huincul's Argentina lizard

DIET
Herbivore

HABITAT
Argentina

ERA
Late Cretaceous

CLASSIFICATION
Saurischia, Sauropodomorpha, Sauropoda, Titanosauria

WEIGHT
75 tonnes (82.6 tons)

LENGTH
33–35 metres (108–115 feet)

BODY
Argentinosaurus belonged to a subgroup of sauropods called Titanosauria, named after the Titans of Greek Myth. They included some of the heaviest dinosaurs that ever lived. The interlocked vertebrae of its back acted like a bridge of bones that helped support the immense weight of the body. So far only five per cent of *Argentinosaurus*'s skeleton has been excavated, but at least some of its bones were hollow. Was this to help reduce weight as it grew to such a massive size?

TAIL
The flexible, incredibly muscular tails were probably used as 'third legs' when rearing up on their back legs.

LIMBS
Robust, strongly muscled forelimbs meant the *Argentinosaurus* could cope well with rough terrain.

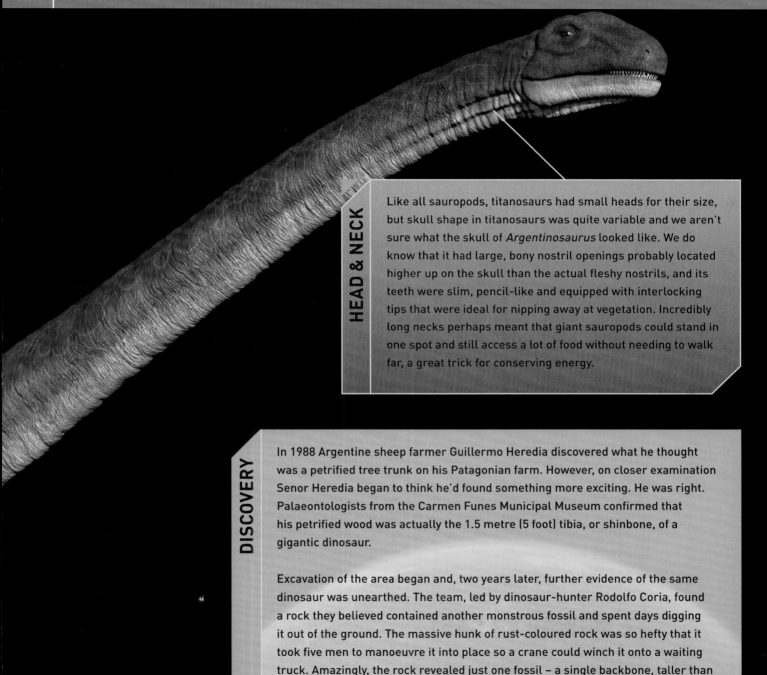

ar-jen-TEE-no-SORE-uss
hu-win-cul-EN-sis

HEAD & NECK

Like all sauropods, titanosaurs had small heads for their size, but skull shape in titanosaurs was quite variable and we aren't sure what the skull of *Argentinosaurus* looked like. We do know that it had large, bony nostril openings probably located higher up on the skull than the actual fleshy nostrils, and its teeth were slim, pencil-like and equipped with interlocking tips that were ideal for nipping away at vegetation. Incredibly long necks perhaps meant that giant sauropods could stand in one spot and still access a lot of food without needing to walk far, a great trick for conserving energy.

DISCOVERY

In 1988 Argentine sheep farmer Guillermo Heredia discovered what he thought was a petrified tree trunk on his Patagonian farm. However, on closer examination Senor Heredia began to think he'd found something more exciting. He was right. Palaeontologists from the Carmen Funes Municipal Museum confirmed that his petrified wood was actually the 1.5 metre (5 foot) tibia, or shinbone, of a gigantic dinosaur.

Excavation of the area began and, two years later, further evidence of the same dinosaur was unearthed. The team, led by dinosaur-hunter Rodolfo Coria, found a rock they believed contained another monstrous fossil and spent days digging it out of the ground. The massive hunk of rust-coloured rock was so hefty that it took five men to manoeuvre it into place so a crane could winch it onto a waiting truck. Amazingly, the rock revealed just one fossil – a single backbone, taller than an average human being. Other remains followed until the palaeontologists had exhausted Senor Heredia's farm. It wasn't much. A few vertebrae, the sacrum – the part of the backbone that attaches to the pelvis – some shattered ribs and the tibia. But it was enough to identify a new vegetarian giant, not only the biggest dinosaur found so far, but also the biggest land-based animal of all time.

EATING MACHINE

From the moment that *Argentinosaurus* hatchlings left their eggs they needed to fend for themselves – the parent dinosaur was far too big to look after them. We know from the eggs at Auca Mahuevo that titanosaur embryos already had miniature teeth well suited to tearing into foliage.

The larger an animal is, the faster it needs to grow. *Argentinosaurus* started life as a 30–50 cm (12–20 inches), 5 kg (11 lb) weakling and yet grew incredibly fast, reaching its adult weight of 75 tonnes (82 tons) in around 25 years. The speed of growth probably varied at certain points in their lives, with a couple of growth-spurts as babies and in its teen years. During these times a titanosaur could put on up to 40 kg (88 lb) every single day.

A MOVABLE FEAST

To gain this much weight, and then to keep going when they were fully grown, a titanosaur would have to eat its way through around 100 kg (220 lb) of vegetation every day. But appetites this size could well have caused problems, especially given that sauropods seem to have lived in large herds. Very soon they would eat themselves out of house and home, stripping every bit of greenery from the land. Perhaps sauropods were constantly on the move, migrating from one area to another to find food, eating as they travelled.

163 MILLION-YEAR-OLD SAUROPOD
TRACKS IN ARDLEY, OXFORDSHIRE.

DINOSAUR TRACKS

In 2002, a series of sauropod trackways was discovered in Ardley Quarry,
Oxfordshire. Dating back to the middle part of the Jurassic, the tracks
belong to around 40 dinosaurs that, 163 million years ago, walked
together. The nearest source of food was over 20 km (12 miles) away,
so perhaps these behemoths were wandering from one patch of food to
another. Some experts think that at times sauropods could have covered
hundreds of miles in their search for food, probably walking at speeds
similar to those of elephants today.

SIX THINGS YOU NEED TO KNOW ABOUT SAUROPODS

1. Sauropods were gigantic four-legged dinosaurs that first appeared during the Late Triassic, about
220 million years ago. They had tiny heads at the end of incredibly long necks. Among the most famous
sauropods are the *Diplodocus* and the *Brachiosaurus*.

2. There were a lot more species of sauropods than we previously thought. The number of known sauropods
has increased by 50 per cent since 2002.

3. Fossil records show that sauropods descended from two-legged ancestors called prosauropods. One group
of prosauropods evolved to a gigantic size and took to walking on their hands, eventually becoming dedicated
quadrupeds.

4. Until recently, experts thought that sauropods virtually died out at the end of the Jurassic period. This view
now seems mistaken: sauropods of several groups survived across the Jurassic–Cretaceous boundary and,
in some parts of the world, remained important right up to the end of the Cretaceous.

5. The first sauropod fossils were discovered in Chipping Norton, Oxfordshire, England in 1841. The Victorian
anatomist Richard Owen named them *Cetiosaurus*, meaning 'Whale Lizard', as he mistakenly believed that
they were from an aquatic animal similar to a crocodile. For most of the 20th century, scientists believed that
sauropods were amphibious creatures that lived in swamps and lakes. Today we know that sauropods were
strongly adapted for life in woodlands, plains and other terrestrial habitats.

6. Sauropods thrived until the mass event that wiped out all non-avian dinosaurs 65 million years ago.

WHY DID SAUROPODS GROW SO BIG?

A number of evolutionary quirks probably explain how sauropods were able to grow to such incredible sizes, although palaeontologists don't agree as to which were the most important.

BOLTING IT DOWN

Sauropods didn't chew their food. Instead, they stripped it from the branches, swallowed it whole and let their digestive systems do the hard work. This meant that they didn't need strong jaw muscles and, as a result, their heads and mouths remained comparatively small and lightweight. It also meant that their necks could grow to be much longer that those of dinosaurs with big, heavy skulls.

ACCESS TO FOOD

Sauropods were quite literally head and shoulders above the competition. Their long necks meant they could reach higher than any of their rivals to snack on high vegetation and thereby avoid competing with other plant-eating dinosaurs close to the ground. Some sauropods, such as *Diplodocus*, are believed to have reared up on their hind legs to reach even higher.

CHANGING ENVIRONMENT

While the Triassic was arid and hot, the planet cooled in the Jurassic, resulting in an explosion of plant life. Lush forests sprung up, towering above the undergrowth, creating a food source that could be exploited exclusively by the sauropods.

OPEN COUNTRY

During the key, early phases of sauropod evolution in the Late Triassic and Jurassic, the world's land masses were mostly united in two supercontinents – Pangaea in the north and Gondwana in the south. These vast, unbroken land masses gave sauropods the opportunity to establish massive territories in which to feed continuously.

LOW METABOLISM?

Some scientists have suggested that sauropods might have had much lower metabolisms than the big mammals that evolved much later on. This might mean that sauropods would have needed relatively little energy to survive and grow, and that perhaps they were especially good at diverting energy from food into growth.

BODY HEAT

The bigger the body mass, the longer it takes to warm up or cool down. Sauropods' bodies were so big that they naturally retained heat. Sauropods might have evolved ever-larger size to take advantage of this ability, which might also have allowed them to be active without having to constantly eat their body weight in vegetation.

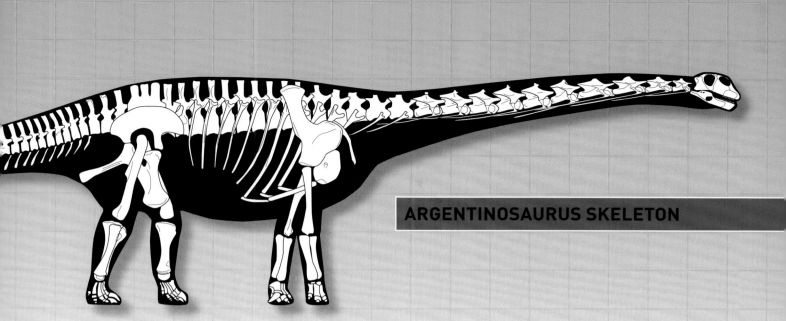

HIGHER METABOLISM?

Nothing is simple in dino-research. Some scientists have argued that sauropod metabolism was high and that they were able to reproduce faster, grow faster, eat faster, and digest food faster, than other animals. These advantages might all have been linked to the evolution of giant size.

INVULNERABILITY

The bigger the sauropods grew the less vulnerable they became. Even the fiercest predators would think twice before attacking such huge creatures. But what if more than one hunter attacked them at a time?

HEAD HELD HIGH?

How did sauropods hold their heads? Traditionally museums and films have portrayed the giant creatures holding their necks out in front of their bodies in a horizontal posture. In 2009, Dr Mike Taylor and Darren Naish of the University of Portsmouth in the UK, and Matthew Wedel of the Western University of Health Sciences, California, argued that this was a mistake.

Taylor and his colleagues examined modern creatures such as rabbits, turtles and crocodiles and discovered that – with few exceptions – most hold their necks in an upright, S-shaped curve. Because there's no good reason for thinking that sauropods represent a particularly special exception, Taylor and his colleagues argued sauropods did the same, habitually holding their necks high, a bit like a swan.

Other scientists disagree with this hypothesis. Australian scientist Dr Roger Seymour has claimed that if a sauropod carried its head upright it would have needed extraordinarily high blood pressure in order to pump blood up to its brain.

DINOSAUR
DEATH PITS

Living alongside giants was a dangerous business for smaller animals. Extraordinary discoveries made in 2010 have revealed how following in someone's footprints wasn't always a good idea in the Mesozoic world.

Ten years previously, David A. Eberth of the Royal Tyrrell Museum of Palaeontology, Alberta, Canada, Xu Xing of the Institute of Vertebrate Palaeontology and Paleoanthropology (IVPP) in Beijing, China and James Clarke of the George Washington University, Washington DC, USA, had been searching for fossils in the Upper Jurassic rocks of north-western China's Xinjiang region when they found three large pits in the sediment.

Ranging from one to two metres (3 to 6 feet) in depth, the pits presented something of a puzzle. The first pit was chock-a-block full of small theropod dinosaurs. Another contained the bodies of nine small plant-eating dinosaurs, four mammals, two crocodilians and a turtle.

That wasn't all. The remains were piled up on top of each other, as if someone had stacked up the dead bodies in some kind of macabre grave.

UNEVEN GROUND

The three piles of fossilized skeletons were excavated as vertical columns, jacketed in plaster and packed in wooden crates ready for shipping to the IVPP's facility near Beijing. There the scientists examined the samples. They found that the rock itself was a strange mix of volcanic mudstone and sandstone. It seemed as if the ground itself had been churned up at around the same time as the dinosaurs and other small animals had died.

JURASSIC MARSHLAND

It was obvious that no predator was responsible for these deaths. There was no sign of trauma and the way in which the skeletons were laid on top of each other suggested that the animals had fallen into the pits one after the other. But that didn't quite make sense either.

Today the area where the bone-filled pits were found is part of the Gobi Desert, but back during the Late Jurassic it was a humid, marshy wetland. It wasn't the kind of place normally dotted with big gaping holes ready to trap unsuspecting dinosaurs. Besides, while dinosaurs may not have been the smartest creatures ever to walk the earth, surely they would have spotted the death traps?

DEATH POOL

1 A herd of *Argentinosaurus* is on the move, trudging across an ash-covered swamp. Relatively tiny hypsilophodonts dart between the feet of the giants.

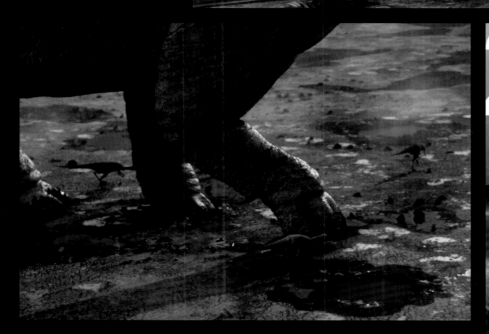

2 Each titanic footfall cracks through the ash crust, creating a massive footprint-sized pit of quicksand.

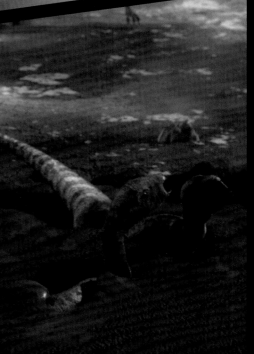

3 Two of the hypsilophodonts don't notice the danger ahead and fall into a sticky footprint. They sink to watery graves as the argentinosaurs march on.

HIDDEN DANGERS

The presence of volcanic mudstone gave the scientists a vital clue as to what might have happened. As the Jurassic period drew to a close, the Xinjiang area was affected by almost continuous volcanic activity. The volcanoes of the region regularly blew their tops, sending molten rock and ash high into the sky. When this fell back to earth, the ash thickened, creating a semi-solid surface that coated the swamp. Beneath this crust lay thick, gloopy mud. Most dinosaurs would have walked unawares over this new surface. But what if it cracked beneath their weight?

THE CROWNED DRAGON

Could the dinosaurs trapped within the pits have caused the volcanic crust to give way? It was doubtful. The largest skeleton found belonged to a species first named in 2006 – *Guanlong wucaii.* An early member of the tyrannosauroid group, and hence a distant relative of North America's *Tyrannosaurus rex*, *Guanlong* ran on two muscular legs and boasted an impressive crest on its head, an unusual feature for a carnivorous dinosaur. However, it was much, much smaller than its famous relative. Standing only 66 cm (26 inches) tall, the primitive tyrannosauroid would have weighed only about 40 kg (88 lb), hardly enough to crack through the ash crust.

THE CULPRIT

A more likely suspect is the region's giant sauropod, *Mamenchisaurus sinocanadorum.* This behemoth – one of the largest sauropods ever discovered – has another claim to fame. It was the owner of one of the longest necks in history, stretching nearly 12 metres (40 feet). That's over half the length of its entire body, which probably weighed in at over 50 tonnes (55 tons) – more than enough to crack through the ashy surface.

HIPS
LIGAMENTS HELD THE NECK AND TAIL
IN PLACE AT THE HIP, ANCHORING THEM
LIKE A LIVING SUSPENSION BRIDGE.

LEGS
WHILE THE BONES OF ITS TAIL,
BODY AND NECK WERE LIGHT
AND HOLLOW, ITS HEFTY LEG
BONES WERE THICK AND SOLID.

TREACHEROUS TRACKS

It seems that, as the *Mamenchisaurus* strode across the Xinjiang plain, its massive feet punched through the volcanic crust. The swampy mud beneath immediately oozed into the resulting hollows, making them almost impossible to spot, but deadly to cross. It would have been like stepping into quicksand. A theropod like *Guanlong* wouldn't have stood a chance. Unable to climb out, and with nothing nearby to grab on to, it would have thrashed in the mud and gradually been sucked down to its death. *Guanlong* had feathers and these would have become clogged with mud, weighing the animal down even more. Quadrupedal animals, able to use their strong front legs to clamber out, might have had more luck escaping. There's even a chance that, as the death pits filled up with corpses, other dinosaurs could escape the quagmire by standing on the piles of entombed bodies.

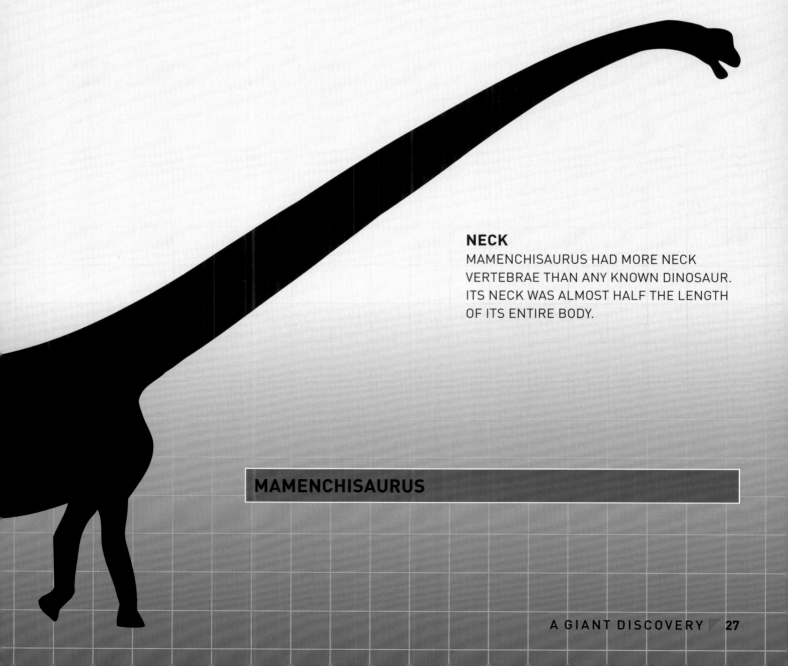

NECK

MAMENCHISAURUS HAD MORE NECK VERTEBRAE THAN ANY KNOWN DINOSAUR. ITS NECK WAS ALMOST HALF THE LENGTH OF ITS ENTIRE BODY.

MAMENCHISAURUS

RIVER OF GIANTS

Some of the biggest dinosaur discoveries are all down to being in the right place at the right time, even if it's completely by accident.

DISCOVERING A GIANT

In 2001 a team from the University of Pennsylvania were searching for a very special site that had originally been discovered by Bavarian geologist, Ernst Stromer von Reichenbach, in the early 20th century. Stromer had written up his findings between 1915 and 1936, but the fossils he had found were destroyed during the Second World War and the exact location of Stromer's site was no longer known for sure.

Knowing the site was somewhere in an area known as the Bahariya Oasis, the team worked out where they thought the exact location of the site might have been, punched the co-ordinates in to their Global Positioning System and set off into the desert.

But they had made a mistake. In their excitement they'd entered the wrong co-ordinates and ended up miles away from their target. Hopelessly lost, they stopped their 4x4 to look for recognisable landmarks. They couldn't find one. Instead, there, jutting out of the ground, was a large bone.

A year later the team returned to the site and, over the next three weeks managed to excavate about 6.5 tonnes (7 tons) of rock. More bones were unearthed, as were the remains of what looked like a 100-year-old camp. There were old boots, tin cans and German newspapers. Was this Stromer's lost dig?

The bones found at the site proved to represent a new species of titanosaurian. As a tribute, in 2001, the giant dinosaur was named after Stromer – this was

▶ *PARALITITAN STROMERI*

1 In the dry season, food and water are concentrated along the banks of the so-called River of Giants. A herd of the titanosaur *Paralititan* approach the water's edge, desperate to quench their thirst. Cautiously, the titanosaurs lower their tiny heads to drink.

2 But rivers are dangerous places. A crocodilian launches itself out of the murky water, almost catching hold of a *Paralititan*'s neck. More crocodilian bodies break the surface of the water. Sensing the threat, the members of the *Paralititan* herd withdraw to a safe distance. Or so they think. Beneath the surface an even bigger danger is approaching. This is –

▶ *SARCOSUCHUS IMPERATOR*

SARCOSUCHUS IMPERATOR

TRANSLATION
Flesh crocodile emperor

DIET
Carnivore

HABITAT
North Africa

ERA
Early Cretaceous

CLASSIFICATION
Crocodyliformes, Mesoeucrocodylia, Neosuchia, Pholidosauridae

WEIGHT
8 tonnes (8.8 tons)

LENGTH
12 metres (40 feet)

BODY

At 8 tonnes (8.8 tons), *Sarcosuchus* was ten times as heavy as the heaviest living crocodile. Its spine was made up of 65 individual vertebrae. The tail was the most flexible part, and the back region may have been specially stiffened. Two rows of 35 armour plates (or scutes), each measuring around 30cm (1 foot) in length, covered *Sarcosuchus*'s back. Its stomach would have contained stones to help grind up the bone and hide that the creature had swallowed.

A LONG AND VIOLENT LIFE

Growth lines like those found in tree trunks are evident in the scutes, and it seems that a new one was laid down every year. Sereno's team examined the armour plates of an adult *Sarcosuchus* that had grown to 80 per cent of its potential size and found that it had been alive for 50–60 years. That's about twice the lifespan of most crocodilians today.

PRONUNCIATION

Sar-koh-soo-kis
im-per-ay-tor

DISCOVERY

In 1964, French palaeontologist Albert-Félix de Lapparent discovered a number of conical teeth, vertebrae and some 30 cm (12 inch) long scutes while mapping a remote part of the Ténéré Desert in Niger. They could only have come from an enormous crocodilian the likes of which had never been seen before. The creature was named *Sarcosuchus imperator*, 'flesh crocodile emperor'.

Though numerous additional remains were discovered in the following decades, the most spectacular were those excavated by the University of Chicago's Paul Sereno and his colleagues on their expeditions of 1997 and 2000. Travelling to the remote spot locals describe as 'the place camels fear to tread', and braving temperatures that approached 52 °C (125 °F), they were rewarded with several skulls, vertebrae, scutes and limb bones. Together these represented approximately 50 per cent of *Sarcosuchus*'s skeleton. It was finally enough to work out the size of this colossal crocodilian.

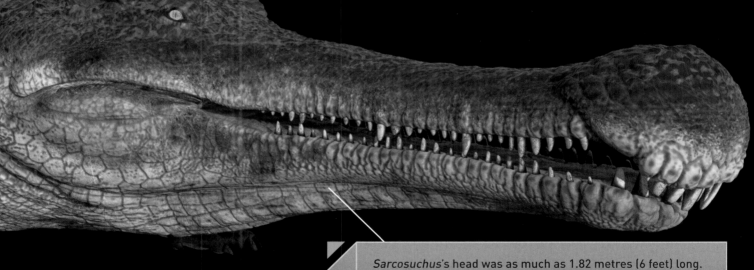

HEAD & JAWS

Sarcosuchus's head was as much as 1.82 metres (6 feet) long. Its snout ended in a huge, bowl-shaped depression located around the nostrils. We're not sure what this was for, but one idea is that it might have housed a large resonating chamber, like that present in living male gharials, which use them to make their mating bellows louder. *Sarcosuchus*'s powerful jaws were lined with 132 teeth. The stoutest of these teeth were only twice as tall as they were wide, so they were strong and good at resisting bending. They would have been perfect for catching fish and also for crushing bone.

NORTH AFRICA

HOW DID SARCOSUCHUS HUNT?

Could *Sarcosuchus* have really bitten down through the thick hide and bones of a dinosaur?

Modern crocodilians are ambush predators. They lie silently in the water, waiting patiently for an animal to swim past before striking, rearing up and clamping their powerful jaws around their prey. Then they drag the struggling creature back beneath the water to drown.

Sarcosuchus probably hunted in the same way. While it fed on smaller fish and crustaceans when in the water, it would also lie in wait to ambush larger prey. Its eye sockets pointed upwards, much like those of the modern Indian gharial. This meant that it could hide its mammoth body beneath the surface of the water, just its eyes visible above the surface. From this vantage point, it would keep watch, waiting to lunge with deadly force.

Paul Sereno and his team have proposed that, via a combination of the element of surprise, a robust skull and a mass of sharp, conical fangs at the tips of its jaws, *Sarcosuchus* could well have been a dinosaur killer.

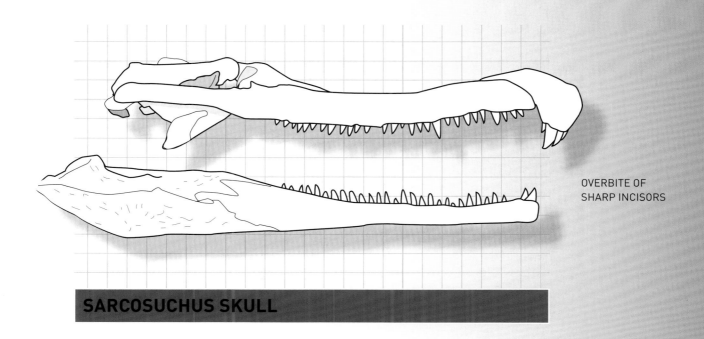

OVERBITE OF
SHARP INCISORS

SARCOSUCHUS SKULL

BITE FORCE

In 2003 Greg Erickson, a biologist at Florida State University, USA, published (with his colleagues) an examination of the bite forces seen in living crocodiles. The results were impressive.

Erickson's team wrestled with more than 60 crocodiles and alligators at the St Augustine Alligator Farm and Zoological Park in Florida. Crocodilians from the park were caught and brought out of the water, and then encouraged to bite down on a bite bar – a 2 metre (6.6 feet) long metal rod covered in leather and kitted out with a device at the end that measures the pressure exerted by the bite. It was a dangerous job as a vet had to sit on the reptile's back while the reading was taken. All it would have taken was one croc to make a run for it while biting down and the £6,000 equipment would have been smashed to smithereens.

As you might expect, the most impressive results came from the biggest animal in the park, a 450 kg (992 lb), 3.6 metre (12 feet) long American alligator. The bite force of this beast came to 964 kg (1 ton). That's comparable to having the weight of a small pick-up truck behind every single tooth in its mouth. It's no surprise that it is impossible to open an alligator's jaws when they clamp down.

SCALING UP

Erickson found that the bite force of modern crocodilians was proportional to their size. This made it possible to extrapolate the bite force of *Sarcosuchus* by scaling up the measurements provided by the living crocodiles. The results were staggering. *Sarcosuchus* would have bitten down with a force of 8 tonnes (9 tons). Once those jaws had snapped shut, prising them open would have been like trying to lift an African bush elephant single-handed.

With such powerful jaws, it isn't difficult to imagine that *Sarcosuchus* could easily have dragged young dinosaurs into the river, twisting its body violently once they were in its grip to tear away flesh and bone.

SARCOSUCHUS

NOT COUNTING ITS SKULL AND ARMOUR, THE SARCOSUCHUS SKELETON CONTAINS ABOUT 250 BONES.

BITE CLUB

How animals – and humans – compare to the force of *Sarcosuchus*'s jaws

Labrador	57 kg (126 lb)
Human	77 kg (170 lb)
African Lion	560 kg (1,200 lb)
Great White Shark	1,800 kg (2 tons)
Tyrannosaurus rex	3,100 kg (3.4 tons)
Sarcosuchus	**8,164 kg (9 tons)**

There are three ways to estimate the bite force of a prehistoric animal:

1. Examine the skull and estimate how large the muscles attached to it would have been. The larger the muscles, the stronger the bite force.

2. It's possible, although tricky, to estimate the bite force of an animal by only its tooth marks. If you have a dinosaur tooth and a tooth-marked segment of fossil bone, you can work out how much force was behind the bite by hammering a tooth into a modern bone sample.

3. Examine the bite force of living animals and scale up to the size and scale of the dinosaur in question. This is the method that was used for *Sarcosuchus*.

ITS SKULL GREW TO A MASSIVE
2 METRES (6 FEET) IN LENGTH

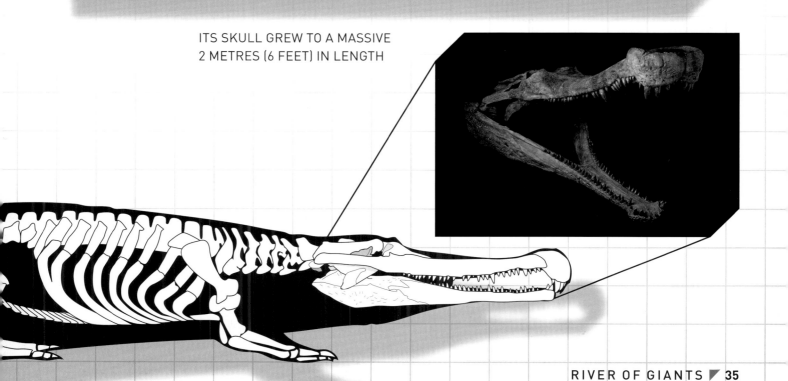

PARALITITAN STROMERI

TRANSLATION
Stromer's Tidal Giant

DIET
Herbivore

HABITAT
North Africa

ERA
Late Cretaceous, 98 million years ago

CLASSIFICATION
Saurischia, Sauropodomorpha,
Sauropoda, Titanosauria

WEIGHT
71 tonnes (78 tons)

LENGTH
30.5 metres (100 feet)

PELVIS
The pelvis of the titanosaur skeleton discovered in Egypt had been ripped apart and the tooth from a large carnivorous dinosaur was found among the bones. This suggests that hungry scavengers set about the corpse soon after its death.

pa-RAL-ih-tie-tan
STROM-ear-E

The rock that entombed the fossils of *Paralititan* was a mixture of sandstone and mudstone. The sediments that formed these rocks were clearly laid down in shallow water. The rocks also contained a lot of plant remains and roots. It seems that *Paralititan* died in what was once a tropical mangrove swamp.

Paralititan's humerus, or upper arm bone, measures a whopping 1.69 metres (5.5 feet). That's about 14 per cent longer than the next largest Cretaceous dinosaur humerus, that of the Indian titanosaur *Isisaurus colberti*. However, other giant titanosaurs would have had even longer humeri: *Argentinosaurus*'s was probably about 1.8 metres (6 feet) long! Titanosaurs walked with a wider gait than earlier sauropods, perhaps showing that they were better able to handle bumpy terrain and might have been better at rearing up, twisting and turning. Like all sauropods, *Paralititan*'s hind feet were rounded and similar in shape to those of modern elephants. Unlike elephants, however, sauropods had giant, curved claws on the inside toes of their back feet.

SUPER CROC ATTACK

1 A 10-year old *Paralititan* has become stuck in the mud on the banks of the river of giants. *Sarcosuchus* approaches the stricken animal and strikes, grabbing its hind leg. The sauropod screams as the monstrous croc tries to pull it backwards out of the mud, back to the river.

2 But things go from bad to worse as a *Carcharodontosaurus* is attracted by the noise. It lunges for the sauropod's neck, teeth slashing through the flesh right down to the bone. A titanic tug of war ensues...

3 ... but eventually the might of the *Carcharodontosaurus* wins out. *Sarcosuchus* lets go and the screaming, lame sauropod is dragged by the neck out of the mud. *Sarcosuchus* returns

KILLER EARTH LIZARD

A BIGGER PRIZE

Sometimes it wasn't just younger sauropods that were on the menu. You would think that a fully grown *Argentinosaurus* would have been too daunting a beast for any predator to attack. You'd be wrong. In fact, it might be that its great size was exactly what attracted the equally impressive meat eater –

▶ *MAPUSAURUS ROSEAE*

SOUTH AMERICA

MAPUSAURUS ROSEAE

TRANSLATION
Rose's Earth reptile

DIET
Carnivore

HABITAT
Argentina

ERA
Late Cretaceous, 99 million years ago

CLASSIFICATION
Saurischia, Theropoda, Allosauroidea, Carcharodontosauridae

WEIGHT
3–6 tonnes (3–6.6 tons)

LENGTH
12.2 metres (40 feet)

BODY

The individual mapusaurs found so far range from skinny youths 5.5 metres (18 feet) long to tough, brawny adults that may even have been longer than 10 metres (40 feet).

DISCOVERY

In 1997, members of the Argentinian-Canadian Dinosaur Project were busy collecting fossils in a rock unit known as the Huincul Formation in the Rio Negro and Neuquen provinces of Argentina. The team, led by Rodolfo Coria, began excavating the remains of a giant theropod, similar in size to *Tyrannosaurus rex*. Such a discovery would have been exciting enough on its own, but it soon became obvious that there was more than one member of the species buried in the Patagonian rocks.

Coria's group returned to the site another four times between 1997 and 2001 and continued finding more of these theropods, all gathered together. By the time the area seemed exhausted of dinosaur remains, they had found seven, maybe even nine, individuals. These dinosaurs were initially thought to be additional specimens of the carcharodontosaurid theropod *Giganotosaurus*, named in 1995, but it eventually became clear that they represented a new species, given the name *Mapusaurus roseae* in 2006. The name came from the term for Earth in the language of the indigenous Mapuche tribe of the area, while 'roseae' described both the rose-coloured rocks that surrounded the site, and also Rose Letwin, the sponsor of the 1999, 2000 and 2001 expeditions.

mah-puh-SORE-uss
row-say-uh

HEAD & MOUTH

The long, narrow-snouted skull wasn't as strong as that of *Tyrannosaurus rex*. Even though the jaws would have snapped together very fast, they probably wouldn't have been strong enough to bite through bone. *Mapusaurus* had sharp, narrow, blade-like teeth with serrated front and rear edges.

CLAWS

The short arms of this ferocious hunter ended in razor-sharp, three-fingered claws.

LIMBS

Mapusaurus had tiny, weak-muscled forearms but strong, powerfully muscled legs. Some scientists have suggested that giant theropods like *Giganotosaurus* and *Mapusaurus* could run at speeds approaching 50 kph (30 mph).

TEAM PLAYERS

Mapusaurus belonged to a group of huge theropods known as the carcharodontosaurids. Already these close relatives of *Allosaurus* had received their fair share of global attention, since the 1996 discovery of the somewhat larger *Giganotosaurus* had led to claims that this 14 metre (46 foot) monstrosity was even bigger than *Tyrannosaurus rex*, the king of the predatory dinosaurs. While *Mapusaurus* was somewhat smaller than its terrifying cousin, the fossils found at Canadon de Grato, Argentina, hint at the possibility of a secret weapon.

The fact that so many *Mapusaurus* skeletons were found together has led some experts to suggest that they were operating as a group when they died, probably during a flood. Some scientists speculate that *Mapusaurus* hunted together, although we have no evidence that they worked together as a pack. Compared to *T. rex*, their brains were about half the size. Would they have had the intelligence to co-operate in bringing down prey? It's more likely that they simply mobbed their victims, bringing them down by sheer numbers.

FLESH-GRAZING

Even a mob of marauding *Mapusaurus* would struggle to kill a creature as large as an *Argentinosaurus* – but what if they didn't have to slaughter the sauropod to eat?

The teeth of a *Mapusaurus* were like knife-blades, perfectly suited for slicing into muscles and tearing off chunks of flesh. They could rapidly approach a creature the size of *Argentinosaurus* and rip away a lump of meat while it was still moving. An injury like this would be painful, but on a beast of this size it probably wouldn't have been fatal, meaning that the pack of *Mapusaurus* could return to slice off another meal as the sauropod trudged on. In this way, the predators could graze on the flesh of their victims without actually killing them.

Mapusaurus may have been a highly efficient flesh-grazer, but any attack on an animal ten times your weight brought its own risk.

DANGEROUS DINING

1 A gang of mapusaurs have been grazing on a herd of argentinosaurs.

2 One of the *Mapusaurus* is separated from the gang and marauds through the herd of argentinosaurs...

3

Spooked, an argentinosaur rears up on its hind legs...

4

... and comes down hard on the giant killer, crushing the life out of the carnivore.

5

The broken predator lies in a pool of its own blood as the herd lumbers on.

SCAVENGING A MEAL

Eventually, of course, the *Argentinosaurus* could have succumbed to its gaping wounds, killed by loss of blood, exhaustion and infection. The rest of the titanosaur herd would have continued on its way, leaving their fallen brother behind, alone and dying.

It wouldn't remain alone for long. Out on the plain, keen-eyed hunters would quickly spot a stricken animal, especially one as large as *Argentinosaurus*. Like virtually every modern carnivore, scavenged prey played a huge part of the diet of any predator. It's too good an opportunity to pass up – the prospect of flesh, even if it's days old, without the trouble of a kill. Before long, they would be flocking around the dead sauropod, feasting on the free lunch and fighting over the scraps.

We know enough about the biology of these gigantic dinosaurs to estimate that a single 72.5 tonne (79.4 ton) animal was made up of:

11 tonnes (12 tons) of bone
3.5 tonnes (4 tons) of blood
4 tonnes (4.4 tons) of skin
15 tonnes (16 tons) of fat
and 39 tonnes (43 tons) of meat and soft tissue.

That much food lying roasting in the sun is enough to feed a whole ecosystem.

IN LIFE
AND DEATH

Wherever giant sauropods thrived so did giant predators.

When *Argentinosaurus* disappeared from South America 95 million years ago, *Mapusaurus* vanished soon afterwards. The same thing happened all over the world. When *Paralititan* died out in Africa 93 million years ago, *Carcharodontosaurus* perished as well. Throughout dinosaur history the pattern repeated itself. It could be that these terrible predators relied so much on their colossal sauropod prey that when the giants finally died out, they suffered the same fate, brought down by their dependence on the biggest creatures ever to walk the Earth.

THE

For almost 100 years Africa was a lost world to palaeontologists, but new discoveries have revealed some of the most spectacular dinosaurs that ever lived. Two giant killers lived here, but how could they have survived side by side?

LOST WORLD

THE GIANT HUNTERS

We've seen how plant-eating dinosaurs grew to gigantic proportions, but what about the predatory dinosaurs that preyed on them? How did carnivorous dinosaurs evolve into such deadly killing machines? What clues have been unearthed to inform us how giant hunters managed to survive and feast in the harshest of conditions?

Some of the answers can be found in an area that has been visited repeatedly by palaeontologists for the best part of 100 years. In the first half of the 20th century, several collecting expeditions made for the arid lands of North Africa and revealed that the area was a veritable treasure trove of Cretaceous dinosaur bones. Numerous partial skeletons of theropods and sauropods, and hundreds of isolated bones were collected from the region. However, these fossils were typically so incomplete and poorly preserved that the animals concerned remained enigmatic. Many of these expeditions were led by French or German palaeontologists and relatively few North African fossils were held by British or American museums. In the late 1980s, the then British Museum (Natural History) – today the Natural History Museum – sent an expedition to Niger to collect new material. Since then, further expeditions have shown that North Africa was once home to some of the most spectacular dinosaurs ever to walk the planet.

During the middle part of the Cretaceous, 93–99 million years ago, two major river systems split North Africa in two. One cut through Egypt, forming the mangrove-like Bahariya Formation, while the other began in Niger, rushed through Algeria and ended up in Morocco, where it is thought to have branched out into a complicated, 250 km (155 mile) wide delta system. The sediments laid down in this Moroccan delta formed a layer of rocks known as the Kem Kem Beds.

Back then, Morocco and the surrounding region was much further south than it is today, almost at the equator, meaning that the area would have been even hotter than it is now. The region was covered by both vast, parched wastelands and lush, sub-tropical swamps and floodplains. It was also a land ruled by giant predators: an amazing array of terrifying carnivores lived in close proximity.

One of the most ferocious was –

▶ **CARCHARODONTOSAURUS**

a huge hunter similar in size to
the mighty *Tyrannosaurus rex*.

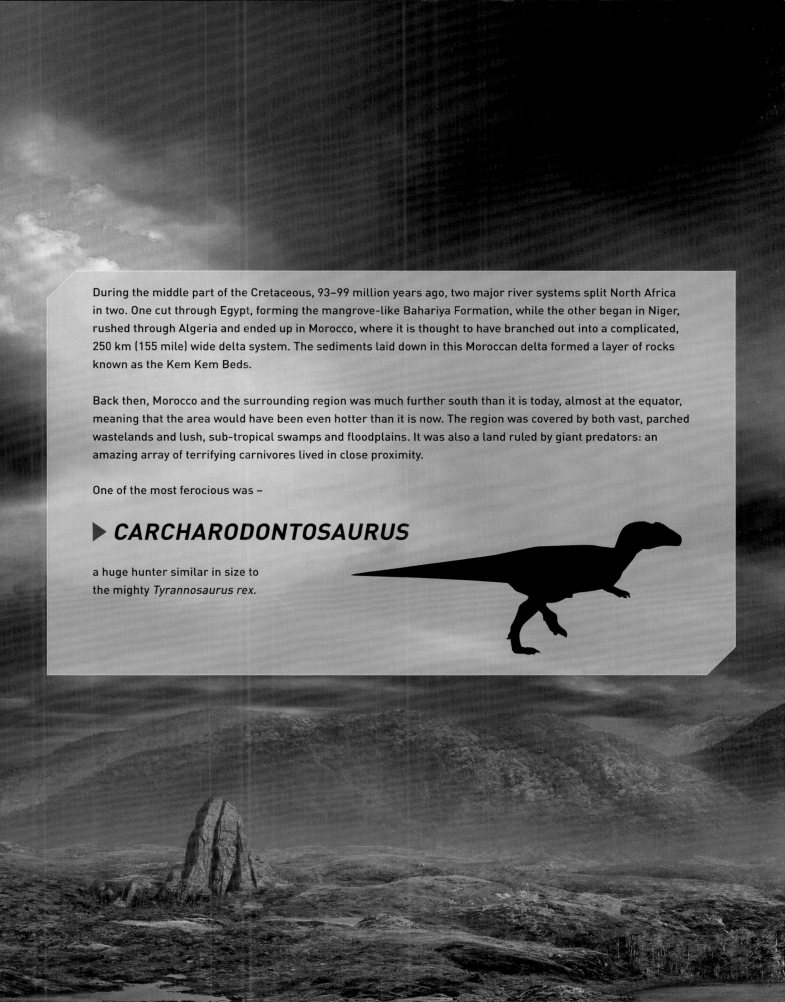

CARCHARODONTOSAURUS SAHARICUS

TRANSLATION
Shark-toothed lizard of the Sahara

DIET
Carnivore

HABITAT
North Africa – Algeria, Egypt, Libya

ERA
Late Cretaceous, 99–93 million years ago

CLASSIFICATION
Saurischia, Theropoda, Allosauroidea, Carcharodontosauridae

WEIGHT
6–7.5 tonnes (6.6–8 tons)

LENGTH
12–14 metres (39–46 feet)

BODY

Heavy, robust bones supported *Carcharodontosaurus*'s hefty body. Standing at an impressive 3.5 metres (11 feet) or so, *Carcharodontosaurus* was one of the largest land-living carnivores on the planet.

THE AFRICAN T. REX?

Carcharodontosaurus has been referred to as the African *T. rex*. But this nickname is misleading. The two dinosaurs, from completely different parts of the world, are only very distantly related and *Carcharodontosaurus* lived long before *Tyrannosaurus rex*. Rather than being a close relative of tyrannosaurids like *T. rex*, *Carcharodontosaurus* was instead a member of the same group of theropods as *Allosaurus*, termed Allosauroidea. Within Allosauroidea, *Carcharodontosaurus* and such relatives as *Giganotosaurus* are included within a family called Carcharodontosauridae.

car-car-o-don-to-SORE-us
sa-har-i-cus

TEETH

Large jaws housed rows of sharp, 15 cm (6 inch) long, serrated teeth that gave *Carcharodontosaurus* its name, each the size of a banana.

BRAIN & SKULL

While *Carcharodontosaurus* was similar in size to *T. rex*, its brain was considerably smaller. The brain cavity in the skull found by Paul Sereno and his colleagues in 1995 (see page 54) is half the volume of that known for *T. rex* and only one-fifteenth the size of a human brain.

The skull of *Carcharodontosaurus* is long and deep. The antorbital fenestra – an opening located in between the eye sockets and nostril – is unusually large. Perhaps this helped reduce the weight of such a huge head. The skull alone was over 1.5 metres (5 feet) long.

LIMBS

The short arms of this ferocious hunter ended in three-fingered hands with curved, sharply pointed claws. It had heavy, muscular legs.

DISCOVERY

The first *Carcharodontosaurus* fossils were discovered by Charles Depéret and J. Savornin in a 1927 dig in Algeria, although the theropod was originally regarded as a new species of *Megalosaurus*, and hence named *Megalosaurus saharicus*. Four years later, German palaeontologist Ernst Stromer von Reichenbach made a new study of similar fossils – including teeth, a portion of skull and various other bones – that had been unearthed in Bahariya by a 1911 Munich Museum expedition. He concluded that the creature should actually be given its own genus, named after *Carcharodon carcharias*, the great white shark. *Carcharodontosaurus* was born.

However, disaster struck on 24 April 1944 when allied forces bombed Munich's Bavarian State Collections of Palaeontology and Historic Geology. All of Stromer's *Carcharodontosaurus* fossils were completely destroyed. Other than a number of teeth discovered by palaeontologist René Lavocat in southern Morocco in 1952, it seemed that the only surviving records of *Carcharodontosaurus* would be the notes left behind by Depéret and Savornin, and by Stromer.

Then, in 1995, a University of Chicago expedition to Morocco led by Paul Sereno discovered a new partial skeleton and huge skull that measured over 1.5 metres (5 feet) in length.

CHARLES
DEPÉRET

CARCHARODONTOSAURUS
SKULL

ERNST STROMER
VON REICHENBACH

CLOSE COUSINS

In 2007, Steve Brusatte and Paul Sereno named a new species of *Carcharodontosaurus*, discovered in Niger in 1997. Named *Carcharodontosaurus iguidensis*, it differed in a number of ways from the remains found in Morocco in 1995 (and representing the species *Carcharodontosaurus saharicus*).

It's thought that both species descended from the same ancestor. At this time, northern Africa was inundated by shallow seas that divided up the land. What if a group of *Carcharodontosaurus* found themselves separated by a newly formed sea? Trapped on either side of the seas, the theropods may have been faced with different environmental conditions. They could have found themselves facing different kinds of creatures. They might have even had to adapt to different natural phenomena. From the moment they split into two distinct groups, they would have been set on a different evolutionary path, until eventually they would both become species in their own right. Even if they eventually met again, they probably wouldn't be able to breed with each other. The genetic differences would have been too great.

This process is known as allopatric speciation and it's still seen in many species today. Nancy Knowlton of Panama's Smithsonian Tropical Research Institute has spent many years studying the snapping shrimps of Central America. Around 3 million years ago the Isthmus of Panama, the land bridge that connects North and South America, was created. Knowlton's team have discovered that the shrimps on the Caribbean side of the Isthmus are genetically very similar to those found on the North Pacific Ocean side, indicating that before the land bridge was formed they belonged to the same population. However, when the scientists put male and female shrimp from both sides of the bridge together they didn't attempt to breed. In fact, they tried to attack each other. The creation of the bridge had separated the population, sending them down different evolutionary routes. When they were reunited, 3 million years later, they had become separate species, incapable of existing side by side.

Two carcharodontosaurs face off against each other, ready for...

FIGHT CLUB

SAME SPECIES HEAD BITING

Many large carnivore skulls are covered in the kinds of SCRATCHES, SCARS, and PUNCTURES that could only have been caused by another large predator

One of the best examples is the skull of a *Sinraptor dongi* discovered in Xinjiang, China in 1993. This 7 metre (23 feet) long theropod from the Late Jurassic stood around 3 metres (10 feet) tall to the highest point of its spine and is thought to have been a distant relative of *Carcharodontosaurus*. The skull preserves evidence of 28 individual bites, each produced by a carnivore of roughly similar size. Some are full punctures, where the attacker bit so hard that its teeth punctured right into the bone. Others are gouges or scores where teeth were scraped across the skull's surface. The marks are so well defined that we can even work out just how the attack was made.

It seems that the two dinosaurs were standing facing each other, their heads almost parallel when the attack occurred. The *Sinraptor* was savagely bitten on the right side of its face, the teeth ripping through its lower jaw and throat. There would, presumably, have been a massive amount of blood loss, but it looks as if the *Sinraptor* survived the encounter. The gouges on its skull show signs that they had begun to heal long before the beast eventually died. (Not all dinosaurs were so lucky. The skull of a *Daspletosaurus* discovered in Alberta, Canada contains the 6 mm (0.2 inch) tip of a tyrannosaurid tooth embedded in the lower jaw. The tooth had entered the jaw at a 90-degree angle and its tip had broken off, flush with the bone's surface.)

In 2001, what might have been a puncture wound was discovered in the nose of a *Carcharodontosaurus* skull, and scientists believe that *Carcharodontosaurus* would have behaved in a similar way to its relative, *Sinraptor*, when faced by a rival. But why would theropods face off like this in the first place?

There are a number of ideas:

HYPOTHESIS 1: LUNCH

Were the attacks the result of one large carnivore attempting to kill and devour another? That's a definite possibility although some have suggested that the truth isn't so bloodthirsty.

HYPOTHESIS 2: FRIENDLY FIGHTING

Is it all just a case of play-fights taken one step too far? Many big cats and other modern predators today engage in play-fighting to learn important skills for later in life. Some palaeontologists have suggested that young dinosaurs operated in the same way. Are these wounds the result of an overexcited tumble with a sibling? While injuries in big cats do occasionally happen today, most of the dinosaurs found with evidence of head biting are almost adult sized, meaning they probably no longer indulged in play-fights.

HYPOTHESIS 3: LOVE IS IN THE AIR

Another idea is that the injuries are the result of courtship rituals between couples. In some modern reptiles and birds, the male will bite and hold the female by her nose, head or neck during mating, sometimes with life-threatening results. Is this what happened here? There is simply no way of knowing, but this remains a possibility.

HYPOTHESIS 4: GET OFF MY LAND

Perhaps the most likely explanation is that the dinosaurs were fighting over territory. Like many carnivores today, it might be that large theropods roamed over vast areas of land that they would violently defend if necessary. It's estimated that a fully grown male *Carcharodontosaurus* would operate in a hunting territory that stretched for up to 500 square kilometres (190 sq miles).

Territories could have been important in attracting and keeping mates, in maintaining safe nesting sites, and even in protecting hatchlings and juveniles from danger. However, the main reason for establishing a territory would be to ensure they had enough food to survive, especially in harsh environments like those preserved in the Kem Kem Beds.

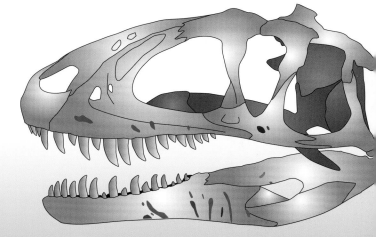

CARCHARODONTOSAURUS SKULL WITH BITE MARKS

We can speculate therefore that, if a young *Carcharodontosaurus* wandered into another's hunting ground, it would soon find itself in trouble. Maybe the dominant male of the area would suggest that the interloper leave by adopting the most threatening posture possible: many living animals use displays of size and strength to intimidate rivals. Maybe the territory-holder would also use terrifying roars in an attempt to get the interloper to move on. If all else failed, battle would commence. But this was a risky option. After all, the invader might win!

BREATHING LIKE BIRDS

A fossil discovery made in the Patagonian badlands in 1996 helped strengthen previously proposed ideas about the biology and anatomy of carcharodontosaurids and other theropods. It was on this joint American–Argentinian expedition, again led by Paul Sereno, that *Aerosteon riocolorandensis* – or 'air bones from the Rio Colorado' – was discovered.

This elephant-sized meat eater, which lived about 85 million years ago during the Late Cretaceous, earned its peculiar name thanks to the fact that its hipbone, wishbone and stomach ribs were lightweight and hollowed out, just like those of modern birds. It seems that *Aerosteon* breathed in the same way as birds: air-filled sacs, connected to the lungs, are distributed throughout the body and skeleton, meaning that each breath carries air right round the body. The sacs act as bellows, pumping large amounts of oxygen-rich air back through the rigid lungs. The volume of air moved around by the air-sac system is huge, and the avian system is about five times more efficient than the mammalian breathing style: this mixes new, oxygen-rich air with old air that has not been fully emptied from the lungs. Unlike us, birds don't have to get rid of carbon dioxide before they can take another lung-full of air. It all helps to make birds supremely adapted for flight, and helps them to fly higher, and for longer periods, than flying mammals (e.g. bats) do.

The lighter bones also help birds take flight. At birth, a chick has a solid bone structure similar to a mammal's. As it grows, the bones go through a process known as pneumatization. The air sacs send thin tubes called diverticulae into the vertebrae, femur and bones of the shoulder region. The tubes bore through the marrow and leave the bones hollow and eventually filled with new air sacs. Of course, *Aerosteon* didn't fly, but perhaps the air-sac system enabled it to hunt more efficiently for longer periods of time. The hollow bones may have also lightened and strengthened certain regions of the skeleton, such as the skull and belly region.

Technically speaking, *Aerosteon* was nothing new – air-filled bones have long been known to be common and widespread throughout theropods and sauropods. However, it helped confirm that a bird-like pattern of pneumatization evolved in allosauroids (the group that includes *Carcharodontosaurus* and *Aerosteon*) independently from that seen in birds.

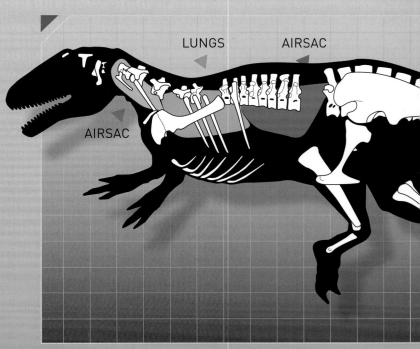

LUNGS   AIRSAC

AIRSAC

HOW DID CARCHARODONTOSAURUS KILL?

All the evidence points to the fact that *Carcharodontosaurus* needed to bring down a lot of prey to stay alive, but there is one last mystery. Compared to the skull of *T. rex*, that of *Carcharodontosaurus* is much narrower and more delicately built. It is difficult to imagine that it would have been able to withstand the stress of holding on to large, scared, struggling prey.

So what was its hunting strategy? The answer may be found in its teeth. *Carcharodontosaurus* teeth are flat and blade-like, and seemingly far too weak to easily bite through bone. However, they do have wicked-looking serrations, just like the teeth of the shark that gives the theropod its name. Perhaps this explains how it brought down huge animals such as *Ouranosaurus*.

CARCHARODONTOSAURUS
TOOTH

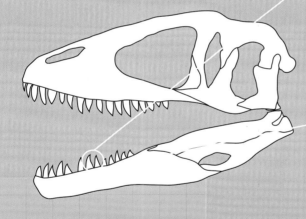

CARCHARODONTOSAURUS

CARCHARODONTOSAURUS MAY HAVE HAD AN
AIR-SAC BREATHING SYSTEM LIKE THAT OF BIRDS

SLOW DEATH

1 A *Carcharodontosaurus* finds a herd of *Ouranosaurus*.

One is separated from the rest of the group.

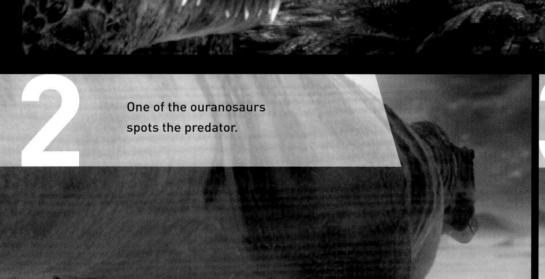

2 One of the ouranosaurs spots the predator.

3 With a shriek, it takes flight.

4 The *Carcharodontosaurus* pursues and delivers a devastating bite to its prey, its serrated teeth slashing deep into the flesh, causing massive trauma.

5 And then the *Carcharodontosaurus* lets its victim go. Crying out in pain and bleeding heavily, the *Ouranosaurus* drags itself away. Exhausted by the hot sun and massive blood loss, it collapses.

The theropod doesn't waste energy chasing the wounded creature. It just stands patiently, waiting for the inevitable.

The *Carcharodontosaurus* finally moves in to feed on the dying animal that is now too weak to struggle.

6

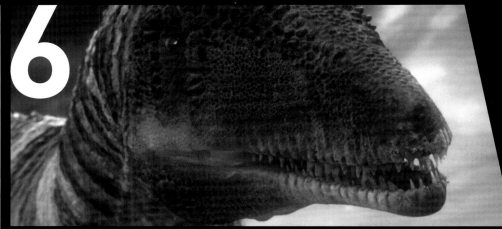

By using the slash-and-wait technique, *Carcharodontosaurus* gets its meal without an energy-intensive tussle.

OURANOSAURUS

TRANSLATION
Brave lizard

DIET
Herbivore

HABITAT
North Africa - Niger

ERA
Early Cretaceous, 110 million years ago

CLASSIFICATION
Ornithischia, Ornithopoda, Iguanodontidia

WEIGHT
2.4–2.6 tonnes (2.6–2.9 tons)

LENGTH
7 metres (23 feet)

LEGS

Usually *Ouranosaurus* would have rested or walked on all four legs, though it could almost certainly stand in a two-legged posture when it needed to reach up high, or perhaps when fighting.

FEET

Like an *Iguanodon*, *Ouranosaurus* had a sharp spike in place of a thumb. This could have been used as a weapon to warn off, or strike, predators. The second and third fingers of the front feet had hoof-like nails to help it walk on four limbs, and its wrist bones were fused together to provide strength and stability.

SKULL

Ouranosaurus's snout was longer than that of its best-known relative *Iguanodon*. Its long jaws, lined along the cheek with ridged, leaf-shaped teeth, ended in a toothless, duck-like beak. Powerful jaw muscles made short work of tough plant material.

Unlike *Iguanodon*, *Ouranosaurus* had a broad bump on the top of its head, just in front of its eyes. This may have supported a gnarly mass of keratin (a fibrous protein) similar to that found in giraffes today. The bumps may also have been used for display or in head-butting contests.

DISCOVERY

Philippe Taquet from the Museum National d'Histoire Naturelle in Paris discovered *Ouranosaurus nigeriensis* during a 1965 expedition to Niger. Taquet named his discovery after a local lizard known as the 'ourane' in Arabic.

BIGGEST
EVER LAND
PREDATOR

A giant carnivore is dying on a dusty North African plain. Its breath is short and ragged and its vision is clouding. It can't see the scavengers that are poised a few metres away. A few days ago they would have cowered and run at the mere sight of this brute. Now, its carcass will provide them with a welcome lunch.

Under the baking sun, the terminally wounded dinosaur's eyes roll up in their sockets and finally the largest land predator the world has ever known breathes its last.

95 million years later, all that will remain of this spectacular creature is just a few fossils, part of its jaw and bones from the spine.

In 2005, the bones are in the hands of researchers from the Civic National History Museum, Milan. They had been hidden away in a private collection for years, but are now sending shockwaves through the corridors of universities around the world. They prove one thing above all. *Tyrannosaurus*, the poster-boy of the dinosaur world, is no longer the biggest carnivore on the block. This monster, which lived millions of years before *T. rex*, would have dwarfed the Tyrant Lizard. It was official.

There was a new king in town – the bizarre snout-nosed, sail-backed

▶ *SPINOSAURUS*

TIMELINE

Amazingly, we've known about *Spinosaurus* for nearly a century. However, due to an extraordinary chain of events we've only recently been able to start piecing together how it looked.

1910   German aristocrat Ernst Stromer sets sail for Egypt on a quest to recover fossils from the North African rocks.

1912   Stromer makes a startling discovery. He finds fragments of a strange, long skull, some teeth and thin vertebrae measuring up to 165 cm long. Could these have supported some kind of sail?

1915   Stromer names his discovery *Spinosaurus*, due to those long dorsal spines, and suggests that the dinosaur would have been much bigger than even *Tyrannosaurus rex*. The fossils are subsequently displayed in a special exhibition in Munich.

1944   During the same air strike that destroyed Stromer's *Carcharodontosaurus* fossil, *Spinosaurus* is reduced to dust. All we have left are Stromer's detailed drawings and descriptions, and a photograph.

1975   A new skull is discovered in southern Morocco, east of the town of Taouz. It is housed in a private collection in Italy for the next 27 years.

1996   Another specimen is unearthed in the Kem Kem Beds of northern Morocco by Paul Sereno and his team. Badly eroded, it is unidentified at first and languishes in the University of Chicago's collection cases until 2002. Here it is catalogued as specimen UCPC-2.

2002   The Civic Natural History Museum in Milan acquires the 1975 specimen and catalogues it as MSNM V4047. It is studied by Cristiano Dal Sasso and his colleagues. These authors also describe UCPC-2: it can be identified as the bony crest that decorated the top of *Spinosaurus*'s snout.

2005   Dal Sasso and his colleagues publish the results of their research, arguing that Stromer had been right all those years ago – *Spinosaurus* was definitely much bigger than *T. rex*.

SPINOSAURUS AEGYPTICUS

TRANSLATION
Spine lizard

DIET
Carnivore

HABITAT
North Africa, Egypt, Morocco

ERA
Late Cretaceous, 99–93 million years ago

CLASSIFICATION
Saurischia, Theropoda, Megalosauridae, Spinosauridae

WEIGHT
7–9 tonnes (7.7–10 tons)

LENGTH
14–17 metres (46–56 feet)

SPINE

Some scientists suggest that instead of a sail, *Spinosaurus* may have had a humped back more like a bison's. The sail may have helped the giant creature to regulate its body heat or could have been used to attract mates.

LEGS

Today we know that, like all theropods, *Spinosaurus* walked on two muscular back legs. In the past, it used to be thought that *Spinosaurus* and other spinosaurids walked around on all fours.

spine-o-SORE-uss
a-jip-tea-cuss

BODY

No complete *Spinosaurus* skeletons have ever been found. Scientists have recreated what they think it looked like from what they know about other, similar dinosaurs.

HEAD & MOUTH

From the 99 cm (39 inch) snout, experts estimate that the skull itself was about 1.75 metres (5.5 feet) long. It's the longest skull of any known carnivorous dinosaur. The snout is elongated and much like that of a crocodile. The nostrils are high on the snout and located closer to the eyes than is usual for a dinosaur skull. Unlike the teeth of most theropods, which are serrated, spinosaur teeth are smooth and round. The upper and lower teeth interlock like a crocodile's.

ARMS

Although no arm bones have been found, scientists think that *Spinosaurus* would have had strong, powerful arms like its relative *Baryonyx*. Powerful meat-hook-like claws could latch on to the flesh of prey.

GIANT
COMPARISONS

The other contenders for the title of the biggest carnivore of all were:

TYRANNOSAURUS REX

Until the mid-1990s, *T. rex* was mostly regarded as the biggest flesh-eating dinosaur Earth had ever seen. Around 30 specimens had been collected, the most complete of which is to be found at the Field Museum of Natural History in Chicago. Known as Sue, it is 12.8 metres (42 feet) long and is thought to have weighed 6.4 tonnes (7 tons) when it roamed the damp forests of South Dakota, 67 million years ago.

GIGANOTOSAURUS

In 1993, Rodolfo Coria and Leonardo Salgado of the Carmen Funes Museum in Neuquén, Argentina, discovered a meat eater initially claiming to put *T.rex* in the shade. Living off the giant sauropods of Patagonia, 97 million years ago, *Giganotosaurus* was 14 metres (46 feet) long and weighed in at 7.3 tonnes (8 tons). It might have been a bit larger than *Tyrannosaurus*, although extra-large specimens of *Tyrannosaurus* were probably similar in size. *Tyrannosaurus* definitely still had one thing over *Giganotosaurus*, however – its brain was twice the size. Dumb though it may have been, the colossal *Giganotosaurus* was thought to have been the largest predator of all time until Dal Sasso's study of the new *Spinosaurus* specimen.

The question is, are there any larger dinosaurs out there, waiting to be discovered?

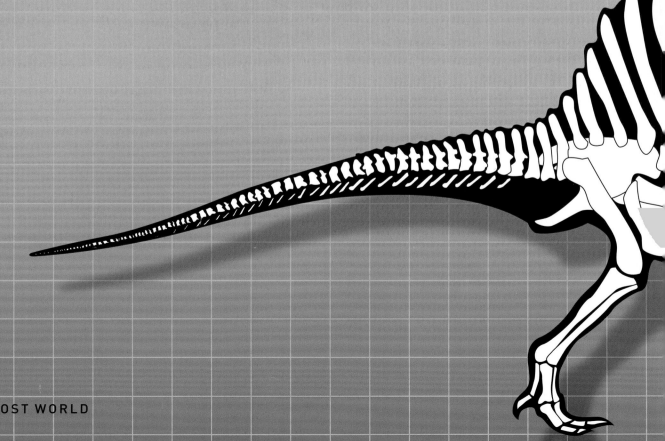

Spinosaurus may be a spectacular dinosaur but it does throw up some puzzling questions. The bizarre killer lived in close proximity to *Carcharodontosaurus* and we know how territorial they were. So how did two giant predators survive side by side? Would there have been enough food to go around?

To answer the question, we have to ask another. While we know what *Carcharodontosaurus* ate, do we know what *Spinosaurus* feasted upon? The answer to that one may surprise you.

Looking at the size of *Spinosaurus*, you could be excused for thinking that the mega-predator hunted a similar prey to *Carcharodontosaurus*: herbivores like *Ouranosaurus*. At 17 metres (56 feet) long, *Spinosaurus* was certainly far longer than *Ouranosaurus*, but it's not likely that this plant eater featured largely on its menu.

Consider those teeth again. Unlike those of *Carcharodontosaurus*, they are straight and conical, without the flesh-cutting serrations found in most carnivorous dinosaurs. Then there are those long, narrow, crocodile-like jaws. We've already seen the skull of *Carcharodontosaurus* wasn't strong enough to hang on to struggling prey. Could the long snout of a *Spinosaurus* have fared any better in bringing down an *Ouranosaurus*? It's doubtful.

SPINOSAURUS TOOTH

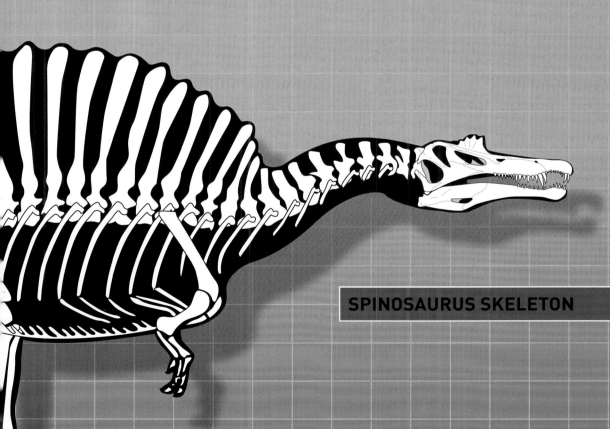

SPINOSAURUS SKELETON

SO WHAT
DID SPINOSAURUS EAT?

EVIDENCE ONE:
The Kem Kem region was full of sub-tropical swamps and raging rivers, swarming with aquatic life. Spinosaurid fossils are usually found near sources of water, and not so much in drier areas.

EVIDENCE TWO:
A fossilized jaw found in 1975 and known as MSNM V4047 has what is thought to be a vertebra of a sawfish known as *Onchopristis* embedded in the jaw itself. Although the bone was embedded after the dinosaur's death, it indicates that the bones were deposited in the same place and hence that *Spinosaurus* and *Onchopristis* probably lived in the same habitat.

EVIDENCE THREE:
In 1983 an amateur fossil collector, William Walker, discovered a relative of the *Spinosaurus* near Dorking, Surrey. Named *Baryonyx walkeri*, it boasts the same long jawline and stout conical teeth as its North African cousin. Remains of a metre-long (3-feet-long) fish known as *Lepidotes* were found in its ribcage – remains that seemed partially digested.

ONCHOPRISTIS

EYES
LOCATED ON TOP OF THE HEAD, THE EYES WOULD HAVE BEEN USED TO SPOT PREDATORS RATHER THAN PREY.

UNDERSIDE
THE ANIMAL'S MOUTH AND GILLS WERE LOCATED ON THE FLAT UNDERSIDE OF ITS BODY.

ROSTRUM
THE 3 METRE (10 FEET) LONG, SAW-LIKE ROSTRUM WAS LINED WITH IRREGULAR, RAGGED-LOOKING TEETH. LIKE MOST MEMBERS OF THE SHARK FAMILY, ONCHOPRISTIS WOULD HAVE RELIED ON ELECTROSENSORS ON THE ROSTRUM TO DETECT PREY BURIED IN THE RIVERBED. IT'S POSSIBLE THAT IT SLASHED THROUGH THE WATER TO DISORIENTATE OR INJURE PREY AND RAKED THROUGH THE SEDIMENT TO FIND FOOD.

BODY
ONCHOPRISTIS GREW UP TO 10 METRES (33 FEET) LONG, FROM TAIL TO THE TIP OF ITS ROSTRUM. IT WASN'T A CLOSE RELATIVE OF THE MODERN SAWFISH. ONCHOPRISTIS WENT EXTINCT AT THE END OF THE CRETACEOUS PERIOD AND IT WAS ANOTHER 10 MILLION YEARS BEFORE MODERN SAWFISHES EVOLVED. AS IN MODERN SHARKS AND RAYS, FEMALES WOULD HAVE BEEN LARGER THAN MALES, WEIGHING 1–1.5 TONNES (1.1–1.65 TONS).

EVIDENCE FOUR:

Fascinated by *Baryonyx*, Dr Emily Rayfield from the University of Bristol used a CT scanner to compare the skull of *Baryonyx* with that of another theropod (a predator alligator) and a gharial – a fish-eating Indian crocodilian equipped with long, narrow jaws. The results indicate that when *Baryonyx* was biting, its skull would have stretched and flexed in the same way as the gharial's.

EVIDENCE FIVE:

Chemical analysis of spinosaur teeth by Romain Amiot of the University of Lyon and a team of international collaborators revealed in 2010 that spinosaurs actually spent a large part of their life in the water – much more than other theropods.

The evidence is mounting. If we believe that *Spinosaurus* lived a similar life to *Baryonyx* – which the fish tooth in its jaw seems to indicate – then it becomes clear that the world's largest ever land predator ate fish!

IT'S ALL IN THE ISOTOPES

How did Amiot's team work out that spinosaurs spent so much time submerged in water? By studying the isotopes found in fossils we can discover what kind of plants certain dinosaurs ate or, in this case, how much time they spent in the water.

Atoms are made up of a nucleus (containing positively charged protons and neutral neutrons) surrounded by negatively charged electrons. An isotope is one of two or more atoms that has the same number of protons in its nucleus, but a different number of neutrons. Chemical elements can have a number of different isotopes. For instance, we find three isotopes of carbon in nature – 12C, 13C and 14C – that are all varieties of carbon (which always contains a nucleus of 6 protons). However, each isotope has different numbers of neutrons – in this case, 6, 7 and 8. This imbalance means they also have different atomic masses, as indicated by their names. 12C is made up of 6 protons and 6 neutrons, 13C is made up of 6 protons and 7 protons, and so on.

Amiot's team knew that a dinosaur that spent a large amount of time in the water would have a different type of oxygen isotope to that of a dinosaur that lived solely on dry land. The team tested a number of spinosaur remains alongside those of other large, fully terrestrial predators including *Carcharodontosaurus*, as well as those of aquatic reptiles like crocodilians and turtles. The results showed that the spinosaur remains contained oxygen isotopes that were more similar to those of crocodiles and turtles than they were to those of the land-living dinosaurs.

It seems that *Spinosaurus* was at home in water.

NORTH AFRICA

STEALING FROM A GIANT

1 A *Spinosaurus* stands patiently in the river, the water rushing over its feet. Beneath the surface, *Onchopristis* stream past, unaware of the danger looming over them. The mega-predator lowers its snout into the surface of the water, the sensitive skin on its snout detecting every single movement.

2 An *Onchopristis* swims too close and *Spinosaurus* attacks, clamping its jaw around the fish. As the *Onchopristis* thrashes wildly, *Spinosaurus* pulls the fish out of the water. Its conical teeth are perfect for holding prey.

3

It throws the bucking fish onto the bank, stamping on it with a giant foot to keep it still.

Powerful claws slash into the skin, killing the *Onchopristis* and carving up the fishy flesh.

4

As there's plenty of prey in the river, *Spinosaurus* can afford to be wasteful, leaving half-eaten carcasses on the riverbed as it returns to the water for more. With the *Spinosaurus* occupied in the river, opportunistic scavengers such as *Rugops* are ready to snap up the leftovers.

GONE FISHING

If *Spinosaurus* was a piscivore – a fish eater – how did such a large predator catch its prey? One thing we do know is that a monster this size wouldn't bother going after small fry. *Spinosaurus* would be after the biggest, and deadliest, catch in the river – *Onchopristis*.

A SENSITIVE SNOUT

Since the mid 1980s scientists have suggested that fish-eating dinosaurs such as *Spinosaurus* may have fished in a similar way to heron. Standing in the water, they watched for a tasty morsel to swim by. But *Spinosaurus* may not have relied on its eyes to locate prey.

In 2009, Cristiano Dal Sasso's team turned their attention to MSNM V4047 once again. Using CAT scan analysis, they discovered that *Spinosaurus* had numerous tiny pores and passages in its snout bones, much like those of living semi-aquatic crocodiles.

In crocodiles these passages are linked to bumps around the jaw housing bundles of nerve fibres that allow the predators to detect the tiniest of disturbances in the water. They mean that crocodiles can lunge at unsuspecting prey even in the middle of the night, when it's pitch black. The sensors, which are only the size of a pinprick, are so sensitive they can pick up a single drop of water splashing into a river several metres away.

If *Spinosaurus* had similar pressure sensors on its snout, it could detect its prey by touch, simply resting its jaw on the water surface. *Spinosaurus* would wait patiently, ready to pounce as a school of *Onchopristis* made their way to their spawning grounds.

Spinosaurus thrived as it was able to successfully exploit a niche in its environment – it was perfectly at home in an environment where big rivers and shallow seas and lagoons were both numerous and stocked with a bountiful supply of food throughout most of the year. With little or no competition for this prey, it was able to evolve to a stupendous size.

Its piscivorous diet also answers the mystery of how it could co-exist with *Carcharodontosaurus*. Quite simply, the two species hardly met. *Spinosaurus* was master of the rivers and shallow seas while *Carcharodontosaurus* ruled the dry land.

SKULL COMPARISON

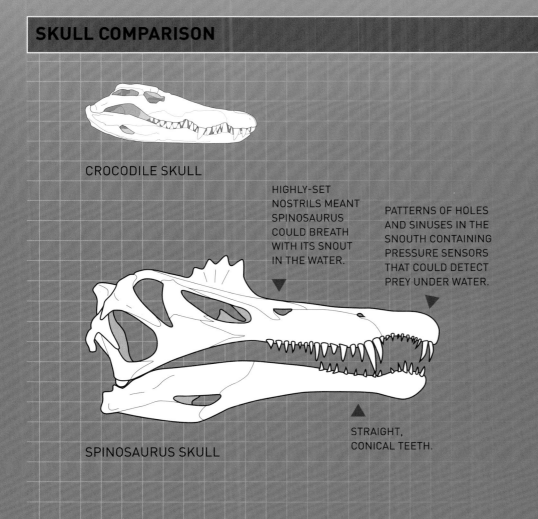

CROCODILE SKULL

HIGHLY-SET NOSTRILS MEANT SPINOSAURUS COULD BREATH WITH ITS SNOUT IN THE WATER.

PATTERNS OF HOLES AND SINUSES IN THE SNOUTH CONTAINING PRESSURE SENSORS THAT COULD DETECT PREY UNDER WATER.

STRAIGHT, CONICAL TEETH.

SPINOSAURUS SKULL

DANGEROUS DROUGHTS

At least, that was the general principle. For most of the time this arrangement would have worked perfectly, but there was one snag. The problem of being a specialist like *Spinosaurus* is that if your environment changes, you can soon find yourself in trouble.

The North African environments now represented by the Kem Kem Beds were highly seasonal and dreadful droughts affected the region during the hottest times of the year. In extreme conditions, the fast-running torrents and shallow seas could vanish within the space of weeks. Where once there was a plentiful feast beneath the surface, *Spinosaurus* would find itself in a parched hellhole, the scorched ground dotted by just a few stagnant puddles and fish bones bleaching in the sun.

At times like this, other animals would retreat to the last remaining oasis. Fights over food would become more regular and, despite its bulk, *Spinosaurus* would have to be careful. It could easily run into danger at watering holes, such as that posed by *Sarcosuchus imperator*. Starving and feeling increasingly weak, *Spinosaurus* might not survive an encounter with the largest and most ravenous crocodilian ever to walk the planet.

Sarcosuchus had another advantage over *Spinosaurus*. In the dry season, its slow metabolism meant that it could go longer between feeding, effectively putting itself into a form of hibernation to sit out the drought.

Spinosaurus could not adapt so efficiently. It needed to keep eating.

This isn't to say that *Spinosaurus* was helpless in such conditions. While it was happiest in or near water, *Spinosaurus* could also prove a fearsome predator on land. While we have no evidence that *Spinosaurus* preyed on land-dwelling creatures, we do know that some of its spinosaur cousins might not have exclusively stuck to a diet of fish.

Baryonyx walkeri, discovered in England in 1983, contained bones from a juvenile *Iguanodon* in its stomach. Then, in 2004, dramatic evidence came to light that spinosaurs might have feasted on pterosaurs, flying winged reptiles. David Martill of the University of Portsmouth and French scientists Eric Buffetaut and François Escuillé were examining the neck of an unidentified pterosaur from the Santana Formation in north-eastern Brazil. While using acid preparation to remove unwanted rock, a broken tooth was revealed, buried deep in one of the individual vertebrae. It was smooth, thin and completely lacking in serrations. It could only have come from a spinosaur. When they checked they found that it was a perfect match for the two spinosaurs known to have lived in the same area: *Irritator challengeri* or *Angaturama limai*. The spinosaur must have been biting down hard on the pterosaur's neck for its tooth to break off like this.

While spinosaurs may well have mostly eaten large fish, it seems that, like many crocodiles today, they were also capable of tackling and killing medium-sized land animals when the opportunity arose. They may well have scavenged on carcasses when they encountered them, and drought times may have encouraged them to attack pterosaurs and juvenile dinosaurs on land.

HEAVYWEIGHT
BOUT

Of course, as soon as *Spinosaurus* ventured away from the water, it would find itself in direct competition with any large, land-based predators living in the same region. And in the North African ecosystem that meant only one animal – the mighty *Carcharodontosaurus*.

While *Carcharodontosaurus* was highly adept at killing, it wasn't above scavenging. Why should it waste energy on a kill if another predator has left the remains of a meal?

However, in times of drought, every carcass becomes a valuable prize. Fights over fresh meat would have been common and deadly, especially for predators as enormous as *Spinosaurus* and *Carcharodontosaurus*.

It would have been the fight of the century.

EVIDENCE OF BATTLE

We do have evidence for a clash between these two behemoths. In 2008, a *Spinosaurus* vertebrae was discovered in the Kem Kem Beds. It wasn't from a full-grown *Spinosaurus* but it was still large – this was no infant. And it was broken in two. It was immediately obvious that it had been fractured long before it had fossilized. So what could have done it?

There are three possibilities:

1. The spinosaur was lying down and it was trampled by a large sauropod.

2. The creature could have fallen, breaking its sail as it crashed to the ground.

3. The bone could have been bitten in two by a large predator.

The only predator that would have dared to attack a *Spinosaurus* was *Carcharodontosaurus* or another *Spinosaurus*.

The bite itself wouldn't necessarily have been lethal – no vital organs or blood vessels were housed in the sail – but we have no way of knowing what other injuries the *Spinosaurus* suffered, possibly as it fought over a discarded *Ouranosaurus* carcass.

1

Drought has forced a starving *Spinosaurus* to leave the river to find food. It finds a trail of blood. Could this lead to a much-needed meal?

2

It has found itself face to face with a *Carcharodontosaurus* standing over the body of a prone *Ouranosaurus*. Taking in the spinosaur's size, *Carcharodontosaurus* starts to retreat, dragging its kill back into the trees.

3

Crazed by hunger, *Spinosaurus* goes in for the kill.

CLASH OF
THE TITANS

END OF AN ERA

Spinosaurus may have won this battle but its time was running out. At the end of the Cretaceous period, planet Earth was radically changing. Climate change was occurring all over the globe on an epic scale and sea levels were rising. The swampy forests that had covered northern Africa dissappeared and *Spinosaurus* was in trouble. It had adapted to survive – to flourish – by specializing in hunting fish. But when the swamps disappeared, its specialism became its fatal weakness.

THE NEW

The Late Cretaceous saw the
last generation of killer dinosaurs,
carnivores that took killing to a new
level. By this time they had spread
throughout the globe – the powerful
and muscular abelisaurids reigning
supreme in the southern continents,
and the mighty tyrannosaurids
dominating the north.

KILLERS

THE TYRANT KINGS

Seventy-five million years ago, the dry barren ridges of the eastern Alberta badlands looked very different from how they do today. Lush swampy forests covered the coastal plains, while the roar of numerous fast-running rivers cut through the humid sub-tropical air, as they rushed towards the warm Bearpaw inland sea. It was an area teeming with life.

That life has left its mark on the land.

The damp, verdant conditions were ideal for preserving the remains of hundreds of thousands of dinosaurs that lived in the area known today as Dinosaur Provincial Park. Since the 1880s more than 300 dinosaur skeletons have been excavated from the virtually deserted 24 kilometre (15 mile) stretch of land that lies adjacent to the meandering Red Deer River, more than 150 of which are now housed in over 30 of the world's major museums. So far, 35 different dinosaur species have been discovered in the sediments here, and many more are thought to lie beneath the surface, still hidden. Dinosaur Provincial Park is a veritable treasure trove for fossil hunters.

However, none of the amazing discoveries made in this palaeontologist's paradise could have prepared scientists for what they were to unearth in the late 1990s near Hilda, an area 50 km (30 miles) north of the city of Medicine Hat. Here, along the banks of the South Saskatchewan River, scientists from the Royal Tyrrell Museum discovered one of the world's largest dinosaur graveyards – a 2.3 square kilometre (.89 sq mile) bonebed containing thousands of bones of the horned dinosaur *Centrosaurus apertus*. It seems that hundreds of these creatures died together, at exactly the same time. But what terrible event could have caused this massive die-off?

THE PRIME
SUSPECT

For millions of years, giant predatory dinosaurs like *Carcharodontosaurus* and *Mapusaurus* were the dominant predators across much of the world. But during the Late Cretaceous a new group of killers took their place: hunters the likes of which the Earth had ever seen before... or has since. A group of predators that took bloodthirsty killing to a new level.

These were the tyrannosaurids – the tyrants of Planet Dinosaur.

Their fearsome number includes the most famous dinosaur of all, the unrivalled king of the dinosaurs, *Tyrannosaurus rex*. Discovered by Barnum Brown in Montana, USA, it's easy to see why the *T.rex* has fascinated dinosaur fans of all ages ever since. Standing 6 metres (19 feet) high, this 6 tonne (6.6 ton) killer boasted a 1.5 metre (5 foot) skull rammed with over 50 teeth, some of which were the size of bananas. Its larger-than-normal brain had massive olfactory lobes, giving it a highly developed sense of smell. Forward-facing eyes and acute hearing improved its ability to locate and track prey.

But *T.rex*, iconic as it is, was only the last in a long line of tyrannosaurids. *T. rex* fossils have been found just 30 cm (12 inches) below the Cretaceous–Paleogene boundary, the band of sediment that represents the point 65.5 million years ago when dinosaurs (excepting birds) became extinct. This means two things. Firstly, *Tyrannosaurus rex* was one of the last non-avian dinosaurs ever to walk the Earth. Secondly, it was the end-stop of the mega-predators, the last point in the evolution of the tyrannosaurids.

While none of its predecessors will ever achieve *T. rex*'s notoriety, they were monstrous hunters in their own right, and the mere whiff of one of these titanic predators would have struck fear into the hearts of any of the creatures that inhabited the Dinosaur Provincial Park region. There were two tyrannosaurids to avoid among the Albertan forest and floodplains: the 2.5 tonne (2.75 ton) *Gorgosaurus libratus*, which used its acute sense of smell to hunt in the dense undergrowth of the sub-tropical forest, and its larger, more powerfully built cousin –

▶ *DASPLETOSAURUS TOROSUS*.

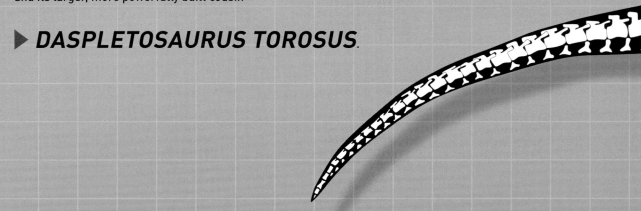

DID T. REX HAVE FEATHERS?

Discoveries made over the last 10 years have demonstrated beyond doubt that the mostly small theropod dinosaurs, called coelurosaurs, were covered in feathers, just like their descendants the birds. But what about the king of the dinosaurs? *T. rex* and other tyrannosaurids were once thought to be close relatives of such theropods as *Allosaurus* and *Carcharodontosaurus*, but we now know that tyrannosaurids were coelurosaurs. This raises an intriguing possibility: was *T. rex* also fluffier than we thought?

At present there is no direct evidence that *T.rex* was adorned with feathers, but the discovery of one of its earliest relatives has shown that this is a distinct possibility. The 1.5 metre (5 foot) long *Dilong paradoxus*, discovered in the fossil beds of Liaoning Province in China in 2004, lived 60 to 70 million years before *T.rex*. Its fossils show clear evidence of a feathery covering on its neck, body and tail.

Xu Xing of the Chinese Academy of Sciences in Beijing has suggested that big tyrannosaurids like *T. rex* may have started life with a downy covering of hair-like protofeathers, but that they lost this covering as they reached adult size. A similar transformation occurs in some modern elephants, which start life with thick body hair, but are bald by the time they reach adulthood.

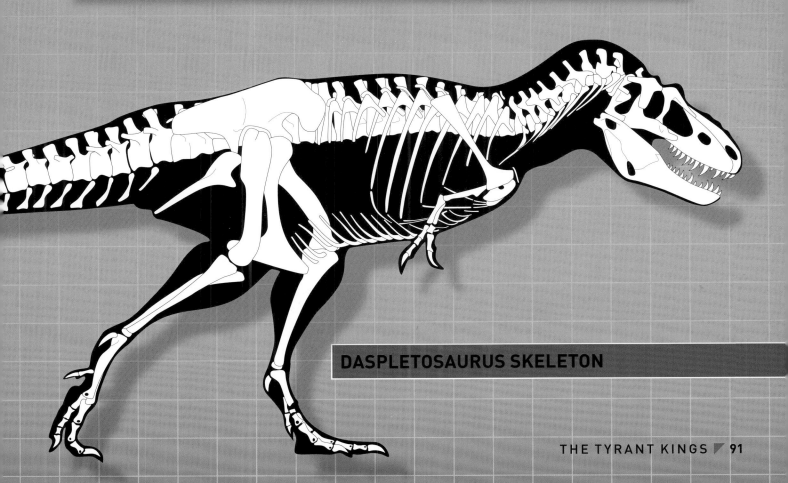

DASPLETOSAURUS SKELETON

DASPLETOSAURUS TOROSUS

TRANSLATION
Frightful brawny lizard

DIET
Carnivore

HABITAT
Alberta, Canada and Montana, USA

ERA
Late Cretaceous, 76–72 million years ago

CLASSIFICATION
Saurischia, Theropoda, Coelurosauria, Tyrannosauridae

WEIGHT
2.5 tonnes (2.75 tons)

LENGTH
8–9 metres (26–30 feet)

BODY

Daspletosaurus had a stockier, more muscular body than its contemporary cousins, *Gorgosaurus* and *Albertosaurus*. Like *T. rex*, *Daspletosaurus* had a thick, muscular, S-shaped neck.

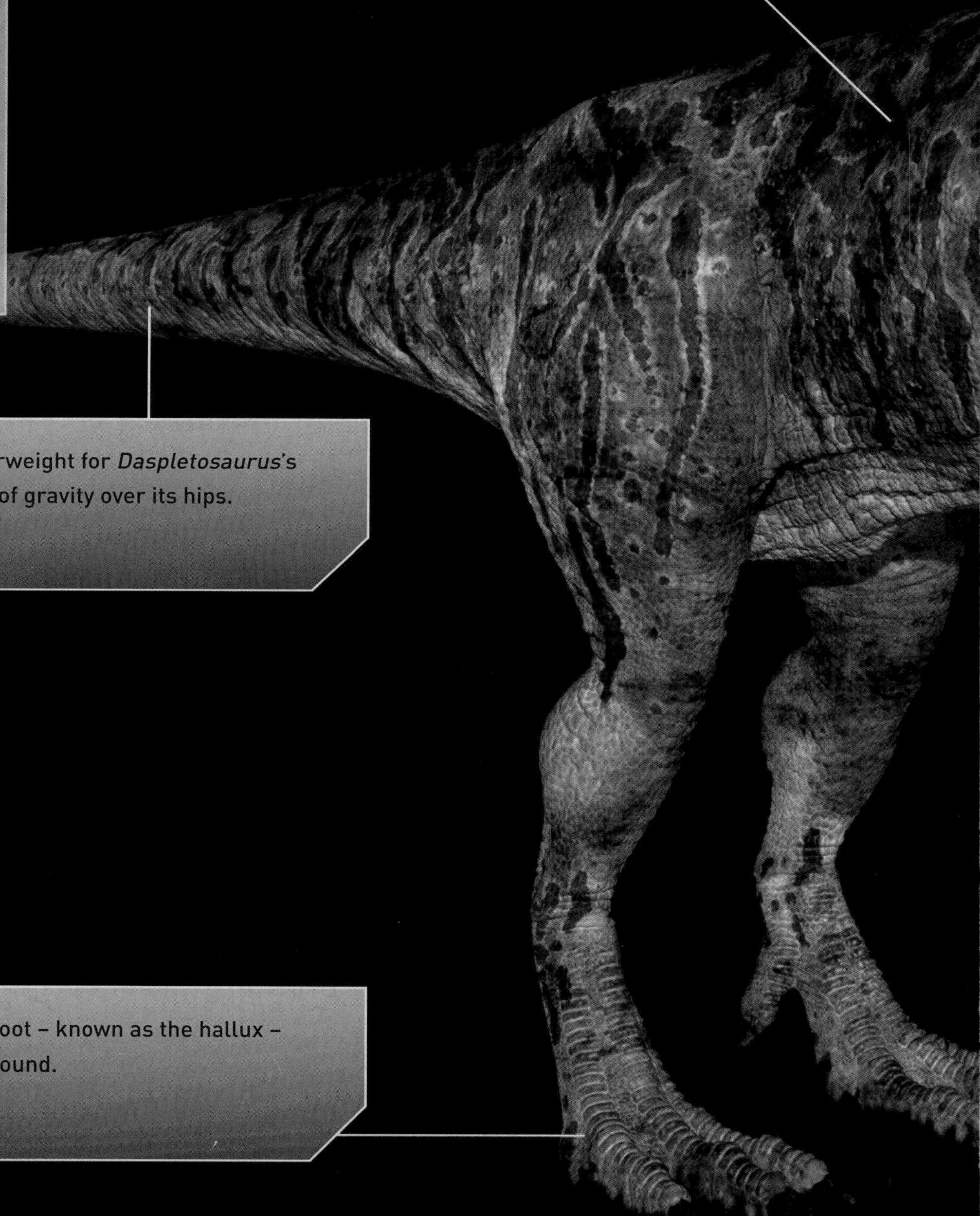

TAIL

The long tail acted as a counterweight for *Daspletosaurus*'s giant body, keeping the centre of gravity over its hips.

FEET

The first digit of the four-toed foot – known as the hallux – never made contact with the ground.

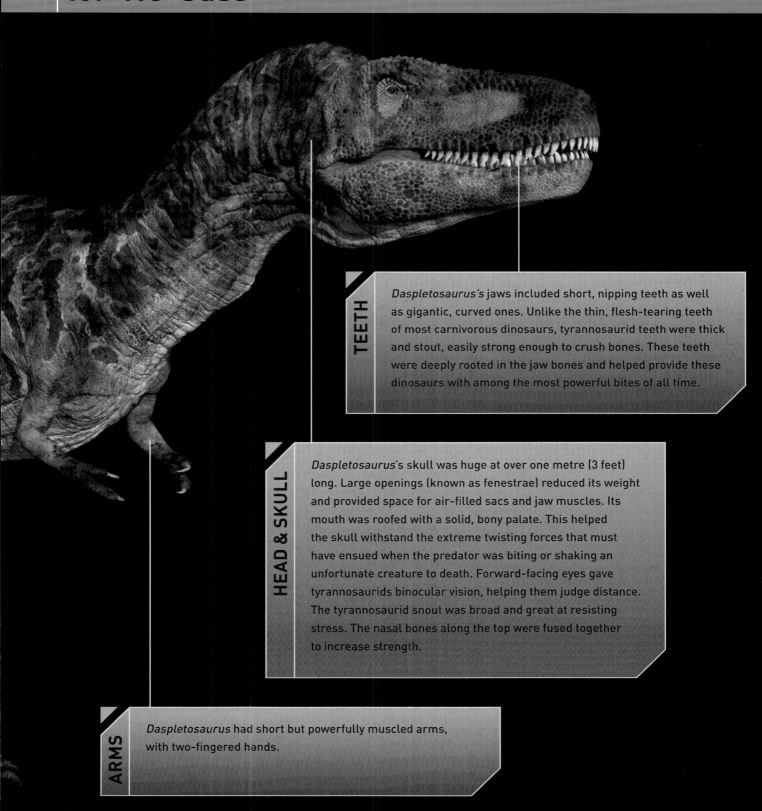

PRONUNCIATION

dass-PLEE-toe-SAW-rus
tor-RO-suss

TEETH

Daspletosaurus's jaws included short, nipping teeth as well as gigantic, curved ones. Unlike the thin, flesh-tearing teeth of most carnivorous dinosaurs, tyrannosaurid teeth were thick and stout, easily strong enough to crush bones. These teeth were deeply rooted in the jaw bones and helped provide these dinosaurs with among the most powerful bites of all time.

HEAD & SKULL

Daspletosaurus's skull was huge at over one metre (3 feet) long. Large openings (known as fenestrae) reduced its weight and provided space for air-filled sacs and jaw muscles. Its mouth was roofed with a solid, bony palate. This helped the skull withstand the extreme twisting forces that must have ensued when the predator was biting or shaking an unfortunate creature to death. Forward-facing eyes gave tyrannosaurids binocular vision, helping them judge distance. The tyrannosaurid snout was broad and great at resisting stress. The nasal bones along the top were fused together to increase strength.

ARMS

Daspletosaurus had short but powerfully muscled arms, with two-fingered hands.

DISCOVERY

In the summer of 1884, Joseph B. Tyrell was leading a scouting expedition to find coal in Alberta, Canada. One hot day, while canoeing along the Red Deer River near Drumheller, Tyrell stopped to climb a steep rockface. At its peak he spotted a strange shape in the ground. Dropping to his knees, he carefully began to remove the layer of topsoil, only to find himself looking at a massive skull. American Museum of Natural History palaeontologist Henry Fairfield Osborn was later able to determine that this skull belonged to a new member of the Tyrannosaurid family which, in 1905, he named *Albertosaurus*. It was evidently a close relative of the enormous *Tyrannosaurus*, but it was geologically older, smaller, and without the specialized, bone-crunching teeth of its gigantic cousin.

Scientists all over North America soon realized the potential for great discoveries that existed in the wild, remote regions of their great continent, and museums across the USA and Canada began to send out teams of fossil hunters to bring back prized specimens. The Sternberg family were among the most famous bone hunters to descend upon the badlands of Alberta. This four-strong band of adventurers was led by Charles Hazelius Sternberg who, with his three sons, George, Charles and Levi, unearthed thousands of fossils. At first, Charles junior hated fieldwork, considering it too much like hard work, but as his own dinosaur discoveries began to pile up, the hunger to find more fossils became his overriding passion.

One of these discoveries was the complete skull and partial skeleton of *Daspletosaurus torosus* uncovered on the banks of the Red Deer River near Steveville, Alberta, in 1921. At first Sternberg thought it was a new species of *Gorgosaurus*, another Late Cretaceous tyrannosaurid known to be native to the area, but other scientists weren't sure. Could it be an adult *Albertosaurus*?

It took 50 years for the truth to come to light. After studying Sternberg's discoveries, Dr Dale Russell concluded that the specimen actually represented an entirely new kind of tyrannosaurid. Since then additional daspletosaur specimens have been discovered in the rocks of Alberta's Judith River Group, but it remains one of the rarest and most poorly known members of the tyrannosaurid family.

It's clear that *Daspletosaurus* was a force to be reckoned with, but could a single daspletosaur really have slaughtered so many centrosaurs in one fell swoop? It's unlikely. The herd of centrosaurs numbered in the hundreds. A solitary *Daspletosaurus* would be hopelessly outnumbered and would soon lose the battle against all those charging horns.

But what if it wasn't working on its own?

In 2005, Dr Philip J. Currie of the University of Alberta's Department of Biological Science announced a discovery. In the rocks of the Two Medicine Formation of Montana an extraordinary bonebed had been found. Three daspletosaurs were preserved in close proximity. Judging by the size of their bones, one was a juvenile, one was a fully grown adult, and the third was an intermediate, 'near-adult' individual. The closeness of these individuals was remarkable enough (tyrannosaurids are typically discovered as lone individuals), but the fact that they were also preserved alongside five duck-billed hadrosaurs proved pardicularly exciting. Geological investigations showed that the dinosaurs had not been dumped together as the result of transport by water; it seems that they really had died at the same time in the same place. What's more, some of the hadrosaur bones showed evidence of damage that could only have been caused by daspletosaur teeth.

Dr Currie suggests that this can only mean one thing –

the daspletosaurs where hunting together, AS A PACK.

If this were the case, perhaps a mob of hungry tyrannosaurids would have been able to work together to bring down even larger prey. Perhaps they could even tackle formidably horned, rhino-like behemoths like *Chasmosaurus*.

DASPLETOSAURUS
SKULL

CHASMOSAURUS BELLI

TRANSLATION
Bell's open lizard

DIET
Herbivore

HABITAT
Alberta, Canada

ERA
Late Cretaceous, 76–70 million years ago

CLASSIFICATION
Ornithischia, Marginocephalia,
Ceratopsia, Ceratopsidae

WEIGHT
1.8 tonnes (2 ton)

LENGTH
4.5–5.5 metres (16–18 feet)

BODY
Over 40 skulls and partial skeletons of *Chasmosaurus* have been found across North America, though some of these are now regarded as belonging to distinct, separate kinds of ceratopsid. Fossilized skin impressions show that *Chasmosaurus* was covered in five or six-sided scaly knobs known as osteoderms.

DISCOVERY
Canadian fossil hunter and member of the Geological Survey of Canada, Lawrence Lambe, made the first discovery of a *Chasmosaurus* in 1898. Four years later he suggested that the beast should be reidentified as a species of *Monoclonius*, and renamed it *Monoclonius belli*. *Monoclonius* is a controversial horned dinosaur, known only from a fragment of frill, and various other horned dinosaur species have at times been mistakenly regarded as close relatives. Indeed, discoveries made by the Sternberg family in 1913 made Lambe think again. The Sternberg clan had unearthed a number of the so-called *Monoclonius* skulls and, after further study, Lambe decided that this frill-headed dinosaur deserved its own genus. After discovering that his first choice of name, *Protorosaurus*, was already in use, he settled on *Chasmosaurus*, from the greek *Chasma*, meaning opening or hollow.

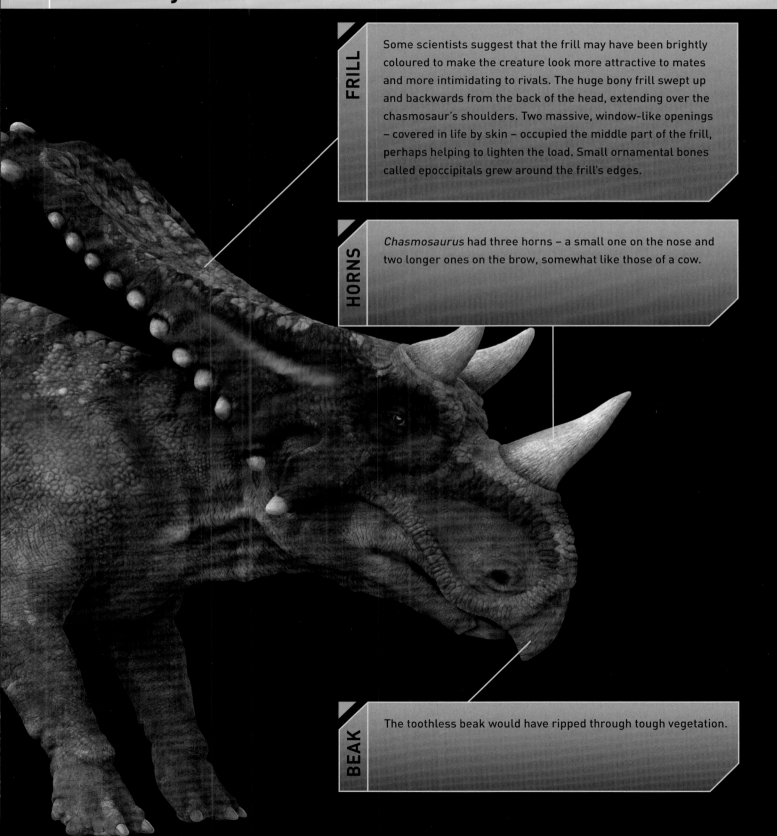

FRILL

Some scientists suggest that the frill may have been brightly coloured to make the creature look more attractive to mates and more intimidating to rivals. The huge bony frill swept up and backwards from the back of the head, extending over the chasmosaur's shoulders. Two massive, window-like openings – covered in life by skin – occupied the middle part of the frill, perhaps helping to lighten the load. Small ornamental bones called epoccipitals grew around the frill's edges.

HORNS

Chasmosaurus had three horns – a small one on the nose and two longer ones on the brow, somewhat like those of a cow.

BEAK

The toothless beak would have ripped through tough vegetation.

DEATH BY PACK

1 A giant predator like *Daspletosaurus* was almost certainly a dangerous foe for a *Chasmosaurus*, but even big predators tend to avoid tackling dangerous prey animals.

But how would a lone *Chasmosaurus* have fared if faced by a pack of daspletosaurs?

2 A *Chasmosaurus* finds itself facing two daspletosaurs – an adult and a youngster. While any such encounter is worrying, the two predators pose little threat to the heavily defended herbivore.

3 But the situation gets more perilous as more daspletosaurs arrive on the scene.

The *Chasmosaurus* tries to put distance between itself and the five killers. But they strike, one after another.

4 The *Chasmosaurus* doesn't know which way to defend itself... and eventually falls.

Some experts think that tyrannosaurs like *Daspletosaurus* may have worked together when tackling prey, but this doesn't necessarily mean that they got on with each other. Brian Roach and Daniel Brinkman note that it isn't usual for animals to hunt in packs. There are a few examples, such as wolves and African hunting dogs, which have highly developed social lifestyles, but behaviour of this sort isn't widespread.

Some animals appear to work together, but it doesn't last long. Crocodiles in Africa and caimans in South America, for example, sometimes co-operate to herd prey together, or to bring down prey and then dismember them. However, these animals don't associate at other times, and any interactions between them are usually aggressive.

Could things have been similar with *Daspletosaurus*? Many tyrannosaurid skulls exhibit punctures and scratches that can only have been caused by tussles with other tyrannosaurids (see page 58). One such specimen is a *Daspletosaurus* skull that preserves at least 50 injuries caused by the teeth of another predator, quite possibly another *Daspletosaurus*. Are these injuries proof that, while these animals may have hunted together, on occasion, such groups were far from harmonious? Was it a case of every dinosaur for itself as they fought for the lion's share of the kill?

KOMODO DRAGONS

GANG WARFARE

There may be another reason the daspletosaurs were found together. To examine this possibility we need to look at the Komodo dragon, the heaviest lizard currently found on Earth. It lives in Indonesia's Lesser Sunda Islands.

Here are a few facts about the way it kills:

• Komodo dragons hunt alone.

• Often, a Komodo dragon will kill larger prey by fatally injuring the creature, injecting it with venom from special glands in its mouth and waiting patiently until it dies from blood loss, shock, envenomation or a mixture of all three.

• At this point, other dragons, attracted by the smell of the carcass, will converge on the spot. A full-scale feeding frenzy will kick off around the corpse as the dragons snap and claw at each other to get to the meat.

• Sometimes, a dragon itself can be killed in the melee, prompting a new battle as the other dragons fight to devour their 'comrade'.

So, did the larger *Daspletosaurus* in Montana kill the hadrosaurs only to face two other, equally hungry daspletosaurs? Is that why they were all found dead? Were they all killed in a feeding frenzy?

MASSACRE AT HILDA

1 A massive herd of centrosaurs is on the move, making its annual pilgrimage to its nesting site on the coastal lowlands in the east to avoid the seasonal monsoons that threaten to flood their usual territory. Deadly *Daspletosaurus*, the biggest killer found in the area, watches from afar.

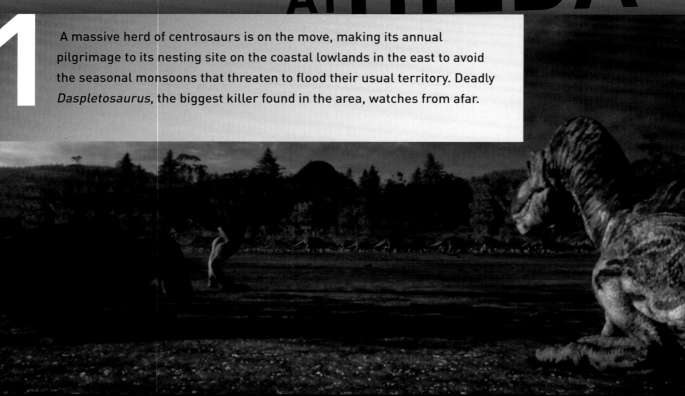

2 The centrosaurs are migrating to escape the oncoming storms but they haven't given themselves enough time. A storm has been brewing for hours and it hits with catastrophic consequences. The herd approaches the river as the gang of *Daspletosaurus* pick off centrosaurs on the fringes of the herd.

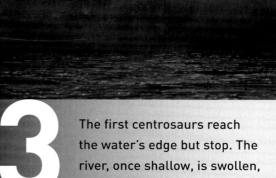

3 The first centrosaurs reach the water's edge but stop. The river, once shallow, is swollen, a dangerous torrent of raging water. No one wants to cross.

4 But trapped in the lowlands, the centrosaurs have nowhere to go. The rivers have burst their banks and coastal waters flood across the plain. The centrosaurs try to tread water to escape, but just aren't built to swim.

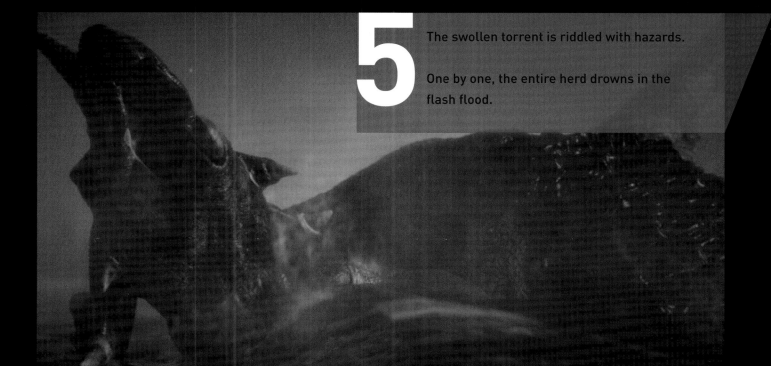

5 The swollen torrent is riddled with hazards.

One by one, the entire herd drowns in the flash flood.

6 As the season passes and the storm waters recede, the centrosaurs' rotting carcasses are deposited across the graveyard in clumps. There they bake in the sun and opportunistic carnivores, no doubt including groups of wily *Daspletosaurus*, descend on the carnage to pick over the bones.

Fossil discoveries in the early 1980s showed that dinosaurs like *Centrosaurus* herded together, but no one expected that they did so in such numbers. The bones at Hilda belong to hundreds – maybe thousands – of beasts that had all been moving together. Even if we accept that *Daspletosaurus* could work together as a pack, there's no way that so many horned dinosaurs could be slaughtered at the same time by tyrannosaurids. A few may have been picked off, but the rest would have stampeded or may even have fought back.

ENTER THE
ABELISAURIDS

Whatever the weather, the tyrannosaurids were the apex predators in the northern hemisphere during the Late Cretaceous. However a different breed of killer ruled the roost in the southern hemisphere – the abelisaurids.

These brutal predators were first described by scientists in 1985 when Argentinean palaeontologists José Bonaparte and Fernando Novas announced the discovery of a large skull belonging to a carnivore they named *Abelisaurus* (Abel's lizard) after its discoverer, museum director Roberto Abel. 'Abel's lizard' would go on to lend its name to the entire abelisaurid family of dinosaurs. These monstrous theropods all shared heavily constructed deep heads with slender jaws and short, stout teeth. Many also had horns sprouting from their dense skulls. Although it's unlikely we'll ever know what these horns were for, it is thought that they could have been used to impress females or threaten rival males. Some scientists have suggested that they were used in head-butting battles over prey or territory.

CARNOSAUR SKULL

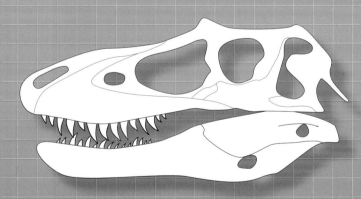

MAJUNGASAURUS SKULL

UNLIKE MOST CARNIVORES, MAJUNGASAURUS'S BROAD, SHORT, MUSCULAR SKULL AND SHORTER, LESS CURVED TEETH MEANT THAT IT WAS BETTER ADAPTED TO BITING AND GRIPPING RATHER THAN SLASHING ITS PREY.

On the island of Madagascar, off the south-east coast of Africa, one abelisaurid was at the top of the food chain. It was a slow but immensely strong killer that preyed on just about everything else on the island.

Its name was –

▶ *MAJUNGASAURUS*

It was thought that nothing could touch it until, in 2003, a study of Madagascan fossils discovered since the early 1990s revealed how some *Majungasaurus* bones were gouged with tooth marks, the kind only caused by flesh being ripped from the bones. Something was eating the island's apex predators?

But that was impossible, right?

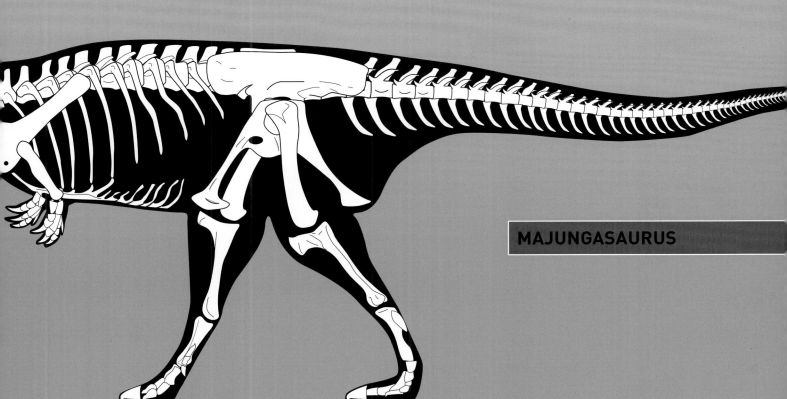

MAJUNGASAURUS

MAJUNGASAURUS CRENATISSIMUS

TRANSLATION
Majunga lizard

DIET
Carnivore

HABITAT
Madagascar

ERA
Late Cretaceous, 70 million years ago

CLASSIFICATION
Saurischia, Theropoda, Abelisauridae

WEIGHT
2.1-2.3 tonnes (2.3–2.5 tons)

LENGTH
8 metres (26 feet)

RIBS

The shape of the ribs indicate that *Majungasaurus* had a wide, somewhat rounded ribcage.

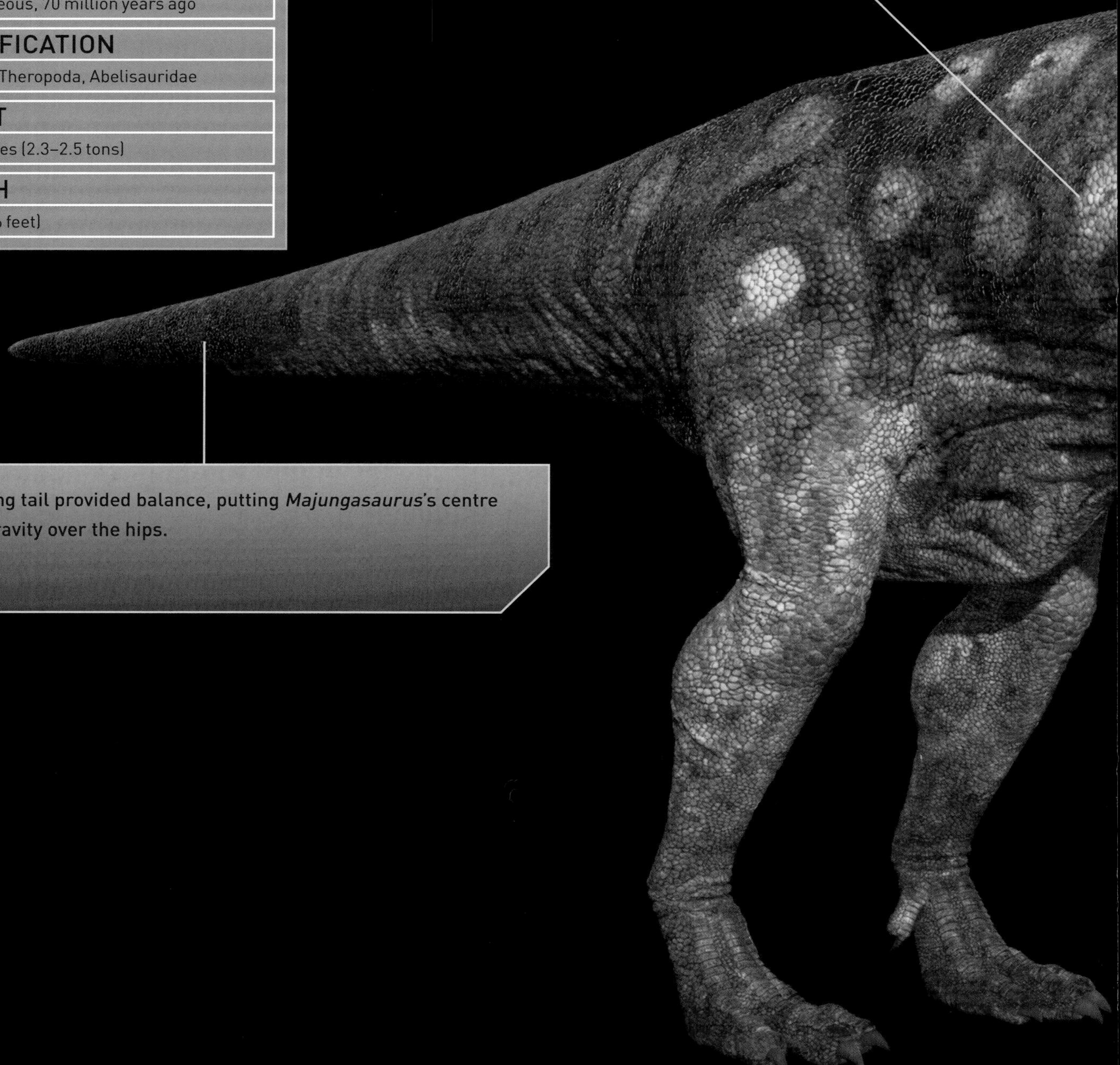

TAIL

A long tail provided balance, putting *Majungasaurus*'s centre of gravity over the hips.

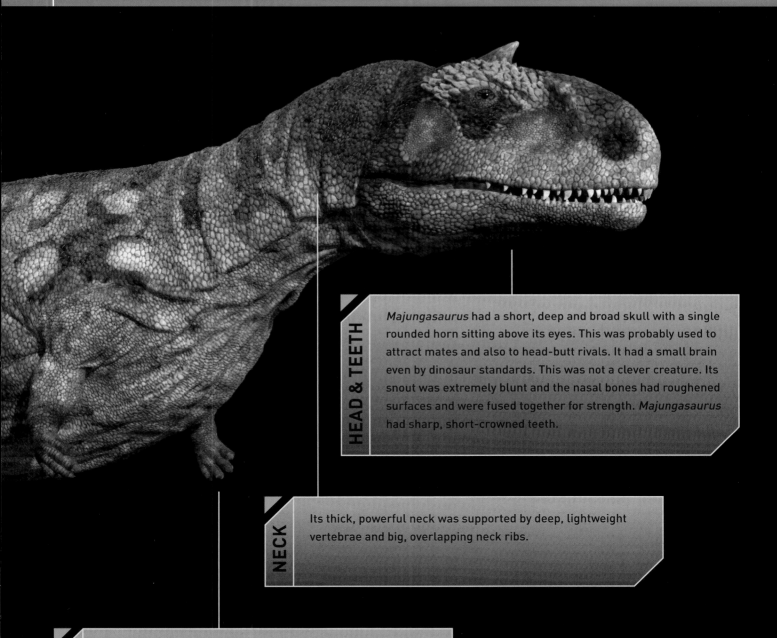

mah-JOONG-ah-SORE-us
cren-at-ISS-im-us

HEAD & TEETH

Majungasaurus had a short, deep and broad skull with a single rounded horn sitting above its eyes. This was probably used to attract mates and also to head-butt rivals. It had a small brain even by dinosaur standards. This was not a clever creature. Its snout was extremely blunt and the nasal bones had roughened surfaces and were fused together for strength. *Majungasaurus* had sharp, short-crowned teeth.

NECK

Its thick, powerful neck was supported by deep, lightweight vertebrae and big, overlapping neck ribs.

LIMBS

Stumpy, immobile arms would have been useless for holding prey. The bones of the stubby fingers were partly fused together, indicating little possibility of movement. Surprisingly short, stout legs meant that *Majungasaurus* was probably quite a slow runner. This didn't matter on Madagascar where its prey were lumbering titanosaurian sauropods, huge brutes that weren't exactly quick on their feet either.

ROUNDING UP
THE SUSPECTS

What could have killed such an impressive mega-predator as *Majungasaurus*?

In 2003 Raymond Rogers, a geologist at Macalester College in Saint Paul, Minnesota, his wife Kristina Curry Rogers, a curator of palaeontology at the Science Museum of Minnesota, and David Krause, a professor of anatomy at Stony Brook University in New York, set out to study every *Majungasaurus* bone that had been discovered over the previous 10 years. The list of suspects was drawn up:

SUSPECT ONE: MASIAKASAURUS KNOPFLERI

▶ A BIZARRE-LOOKING THEROPOD NAMED IN 2001 BY PALAEONTOLOGIST SCOTT SAMPSON

Weighing around 40 kg (88 lb), this 2 metre (6.6 foot) long carnivore had unusual lower front teeth that jutted out almost horizontally from its lower jaw. But there was no way a creature the weight of a large dog could bring down a monster four times its size. Neither did the peculiar teeth match the scars on the skulls.

VERDICT: NOT GUILTY

SUSPECT TWO: MAHAJANGASUCHUS INSIGNIS

▶ A LARGE CROCODILIAN FIRST DISCOVERED IN 1998

It had a head full of blunt, conical teeth that it would clamp around prey. They were certainly robust, but just too blunt to cause the kind of damage found in the majungasaurs.

VERDICT: NOT GUILTY

SUSPECT THREE: TREMATOCHAMPSA OBLITA

▶ ANOTHER PARTICULARLY NASTY PREHISTORIC CROC

Like the *Mahajangasuchus*, *Trematochampsa*'s teeth were too irregularly spaced and variable in height, size and orientation to match the extremely evenly spaced tooth marks found on the fossils. Neither crocodilian had the kind of serrated teeth that could create some of the score marks that scientists have found on the best-preserved *Majungasaurus* fossils.

VERDICT: NOT GUILTY

One by one, the suspects were eliminated from the investigation. And then the horrible truth was revealed. Nothing on Madagascar could have slaughtered and stripped the *Majungasaurus* of its flesh – nothing except *Majungasaurus* itself.

DESPERATE
TIMES

Scientists had long suspected that dinosaurs indulged in cannibalism, but it had never been proved. Now there was cold, hard proof. But what could cause a killer as efficient as *Majungasaurus* to turn on its own species? The answer is simple. It was starving. Even 70 million years ago, Madagascar was an island, but it was much hotter than it is today. While there were occasional floods, the inhabitants of the island often faced terrible droughts that could have lasted months. Mighty rivers would become trickles and watering holes soon dried up. *Majungasaurus* may have been the apex-predator, but what do you eat when all your prey starts dying of thirst? There's no other choice. Once you've exhausted the arid plains, stripping the flesh off every last bone, the only thing left to eat is your own kind, maybe even your own family.

CANNIBALISM TODAY

Believe it or not, many of today's animals are cannibals. Among the creatures that regularly dine out on members of their own species are:

- Chimpanzees
- Rattlesnakes
- Komodo dragons
- Red foxes
- Lions
- Tiger salamanders

MAJUNGASAURUS YOUNG AND THEIR
MOTHER FEED ON THEIR OWN KIND

CANNIBAL
TERROR

MADAGASCAR

POLAR DINOSAURS

Whether hunting in packs or turning on their own kin, the most successful predators in the modern world are generalists able to adapt to diverse environments and make a living in all kinds of different habitats. In the frozen north of the Late Cretaceous world, that's exactly what one rather surprising hunter did. When most people think of dinosaur bones, they conjure up images of the badlands of America or the dunes of deserts. The unforgiving frozen wastes of Alaska are the last place they think of looking.

For most of the 20th century palaeontologists largely ignored the rocks that, during Mesozoic times, were laid down within the Arctic Circle. It was considered unlikely that dinosaurs could have survived in such conditions. However, fossils were found from time to time, such as those discovered by geologist Robert Liscomb in 1961. The remains were found during a Shell Oil survey near the Colville River in the most northern tip of Alaska, known as North Slope. Thinking that these fossils belonged to Ice Age creatures that dated back a mere two million years, Liscomb sent them back to his office and planned to have them analysed at a later date. Sadly, one year later, Liscomb was killed in a rockslide, so his fossils languished unidentified in a warehouse for the next 25 years.

In the mid-1980s, Shell employees decided to clear out the warehouse and rediscovered the bones in the box where they had lain untouched for decades. Shell sent them to the United States Geological Survey, where palaeontologist Charles Repenning immediately identified them as dinosaur remains, namely a duck-billed dinosaur by the name of *Edmontosaurus*.

Around the same time Henry Roehler and Gary Stricker of the US Geological Survey were finding other fragments of dinosaurs across north-western Alaska, including fossilized skin impressions. The evidence was mounting. Dinosaurs did roam Alaska, 75 to 70 million years ago, a mere five million years before dinosaurs (excepting birds, of course) were wiped out.

75 millions years ago, Alaska was nearer to the North Pole than it is today. While the temperature would have been warmer than today, life would still have been tough for the dinosaurs who braved the winter months. Today, due to the axis of the Earth, the North Slope of Alaska enjoys a month of constant daylight when the North Pole is facing the sun. Come winter, when the North Pole tilts away from the sun, northern Alaska is plunged into six weeks of almost total darkness. Back in the Late Cretaceous, the change in season was far more dramatic.

NORTH ALASKA NOW AND THEN

	NOW	THEN
DISTANCE TO THE NORTH POLE	1,500 miles	350 miles
CLIMATE	High 38 °F (3.3 °C) Low 34 °F (1 °C)	High 55 °F (13 °C) Low 37 °F (3 °C)
HABITAT	Snow-covered tundra	Cover of coniferous trees that lost their leaves in winter, with understorey of flowering plants and ferns
WINTER	6 weeks of near total darkness	4 months of near total darkness

EDMONTOSAURUS REGALIS

TRANSLATION
King-sized lizard from Edmonton

DIET
Herbivore

HABITAT
North America

ERA
Late Cretaceous, 71–65 million years ago

CLASSIFICATION
Ornithischia, Ornithopoda, Iguanodontia, Hadrosauridae

WEIGHT
3.7 tonnes (4 tons)

LENGTH
9 metres (30 feet)

BODY & SPINE

Edmontosaurus's spine curved down at the shoulders, and the neck was long and flexible, suggesting that it was well-suited to keeping its head low to the ground where it could graze on small, low-growing plants – useful in environments where foliage was rare. Fossilized skin shows that *Edmontosaurus* was covered in a leathery, scaly hide. A soft crest grew along the top of its neck, back and tail.

DISCOVERY

Edmontosaurus has a long and complicated history. The first remains were discovered in 1891 in Wyoming, USA. A year later Othniel Charles Marsh named them *Claosaurus annectens* (he had previously named *Claosaurus* for a species termed *Claosaurus agilis*, but other scientists argued about his classification. Many hadrosaurs had been named for fragmentary remains and experts disagreed as to which were truly distinct, and which were the same, but wrongly named. Some used the name *Diclonius* for *Claosaurus annectans* while others argued that it should be identified as a species of *thespesius* or *Trachodon*. Both these names had also been raised for fragmentary remains very similar to those of *Diclonius* and *Claosaurus*. In 1917 Lawrence Lambe made a new study of the bones alongside two partial skeletons that had been found in the Edmonton Formation in Alberta, Canada. Lambe named the new genus and species *Edmontosaurus regalis*, and it was eventually shown that *Claosaurus annectens* was also a species of *Edmontosaurus*. Today, Marsh's original specimen is known as *Edmontosaurus annectans*. It remains impossible to work out exactly which hadrosaurs the more fragmentary bits and pieces truly belong to.

PRONUNCIATION

ed-MON-to-SORE-uss
Reg-al-iss

HEAD

The skull of an adult *Edmontosaurus* was around one metre (3 feet) long. In contrast to some other hadrosaurs, it lacked a bony crest on its head. Muscular cheeks on the outside of its jaws stored chewed plant material inside the mouth prior to swallowing.

NOSE & MOUTH

Enormous nostrils were surrounded by concave depressions. These could have housed fleshy folds of loose skin that might have formed balloon-like sacs when blasted full of air. These could have been used to make bellowing noises to attract mates or warning sounds for the herd. *Edmontosaurus*'s tough, duckbilled beak would have been used to rip through shrubs and plants. While it was toothless, its long jaws contained tightly packed tooth batteries containing an amazing thousand or so tiny teeth. As teeth broke off or became worn down, new ones grew in their place.

LEGS

Strong hind legs meant they could stand on their back legs to reach foliage on trees overhead. Most of the time they walked on all fours, although their front legs were shorter than their back ones. Hoofed feet supported the mammoth body.

WOUNDED
TEETH

While some species of *Edmontosaurus* found in more southern climes had to deal with the attention of the *Tyrannosaurus rex*, those from Alaska faced a much smaller predator –

▶ *TROODON FORMOSUS*

In 1856, scientist Joseph Leidy examined a single leaf-shaped serrated tooth and named it *Troodon formosus*, meaning wounded teeth. However, at that time dinosaur discoveries in North America were rare and Leidy thought he was dealing with a fossil lizard. Nearly 50 years later, in 1901, scientists realized that *Troodon* was, in fact, a dinosaur. However, they still had no idea what kind of dinosaur it was as no other bones had been found.

In the early 1930s, *Troodon* remains were finally unearthed in Alberta – pieces of a hand, foot and tail. After studying these fossils, Charles R. Sternberg regarded them as representing a new kind of bird-like theropod that he called *Stenonychosaurus*. It would be another 50 years before additional work showed that *Stenonychosaurus* was actually the same animal as *Troodon*. Because the name *Troodon* had been published first, it had to be used in favour of *Stenonychosaurus*.

Arguments about what is and what isn't a *Troodon* still rage as the fossils of this troublesome dinosaur are so widespread. *Troodon* fossils have been found all across North America, from Alaska in the north to Texas and New Mexico in the south. Supposedly widespread dinosaurs like this often cause palaeontologists to question whether every single discovery truly belongs to the same genus.

TROODON SKELETON

THE WORLD'S BRAINIEST DINO

While experts might disagree about names and species, they all agree that *Troodon* was an intelligent dinosaur. *Troodon* skulls reveal that the animal had (for a dinosaur) a peculiarly large brain, much bigger in proportion to its body than other Mesozoic dinosaurs its size. Scientists work out how intelligent a dinosaur might have been by a formula known as the encephalizaton quotient, or EQ scale. This compares the weight of its brain to the weight of its body. This ratio is then contrasted with that of other creatures. An EQ of 2.0 means that an animal's brain was twice as heavy as another animal's with a similar weight.

Our human brains score an impressive 5.07 to 8.0 (depending on which EQ scale you are using), higher than virtually all (but not all) other animals. Nearest to us are the bottlenose dolphin at 3.60 and capuchin monkeys at 2.52. An African elephant lumbers onto the scale at 0.68 while the Hippopotamus weighs in at a mere 0.27.

Dinosaurs generally don't do well when it comes to EQ. *Triceratops* scrapes in with an EQ of 0.2 while giant sauropods like *Giraffatitan* just about muster a 0.1. *Troodon* however is a veritable genius with an EQ of 0.8. Their Alaskan prey, *Edmontosaurus*, probably had an EQ around 0.47.

TROODON FORMOSUS

TRANSLATION
Beautifully crafted wounded tooth

DIET
Omnivore

HABITAT
North America, Canada, Alaska

ERA
Late Cretaceous, 71–65 million years ago

CLASSIFICATION
Saurischia, Theropoda, Coelurosauria,
Maniraptoran, Troodontidae

WEIGHT
100 kg (220 lb)

LENGTH
4 metres (13 feet)

BODY
Beautifully preserved close relatives of *Troodon* from China show that all of these bird-like dinosaurs were fully covered in feathers. This would have been essential for those *Troodon* that lived in the cold, frozen Arctic north.

PATERNAL CARE
As well as many, many teeth, scientists have discovered a large number of fossilized *Troodon* nests in the Campanian Two Medicine Formation of Montana. These nests contained *Troodon* eggs, and at least some of these eggs contained embryos. This means we know a surprising amount about how *Troodon* reproduced. *Troodon* laid approximately two eggs every day until it had a clutch of 24 eggs packed tightly in the nest. One or both of the parents then sat on top of the nest, either to help keep it warm or to guard it from predators. Some experts have argued that it was the male *Troodon* that took on the brooding job, not the mother, who could have been off hunting while the dad guarded the next generation.

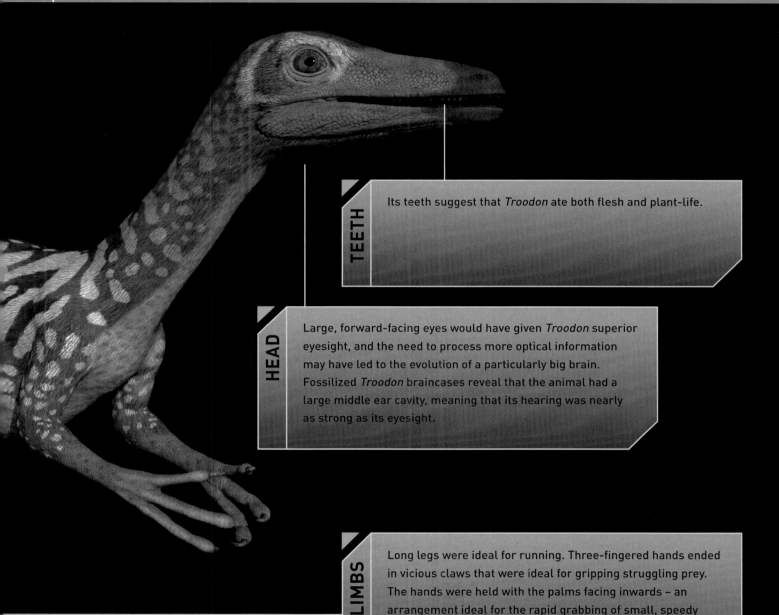

TEETH

Its teeth suggest that *Troodon* ate both flesh and plant-life.

HEAD

Large, forward-facing eyes would have given *Troodon* superior eyesight, and the need to process more optical information may have led to the evolution of a particularly big brain. Fossilized *Troodon* braincases reveal that the animal had a large middle ear cavity, meaning that its hearing was nearly as strong as its eyesight.

LIMBS

Long legs were ideal for running. Three-fingered hands ended in vicious claws that were ideal for gripping struggling prey. The hands were held with the palms facing inwards – an arrangement ideal for the rapid grabbing of small, speedy prey. The large, sickle-shaped claw on its second toe was kept off the ground during running and could have caused serious damage during attacks.

BODY BUILDERS

In 2008, Tony Fiorillo of the Museum of Nature and Science in Dallas studied a number of *Troodon* teeth that had been discovered near the Colville River in Alaska's North Slope. When he compared them with *Troodon formosus* teeth previously discovered in Alberta and Montana he realized that the Alaskan fossils were 50 per cent bigger than those of their southern cousins. As tooth size usually relates to body size, Fiorillo estimated that the Alaskan *Troodons* were about twice the size of those found in the lower states.

By comparing the wear and tear on both Alaskan and southern *Troodon*, Fiorillo worked out that both populations ate the same kind of food, a mixture of meat and plant-life. So why did the northern *Troodon* grow so big?

SLEEPING GIANTS

Alaska during the Late Cretaceous was an even tougher environment than it is today. Winter nights were cold and long, lasting months at a time. Hadrosaurs such as *Edmontosaurus* probably didn't migrate out of the area during cold spells, especially if they had youngsters in the herd that would have been too small to make any long journeys.

During the long, bright days, the bulky hadrosaurs would have had little to fear from *Troodon*. Instead, they would have kept an eye out for larger hunters such as the 10 metre (3 feet) long *Gorgosaurus*.

However, when night fell it was a different story.

THE EYES HAVE IT

As well as a large brain, *Troodon* had exceptionally large eyes for an animal of its size. In modern animals, large eyes usually mean that creatures can see well in low-light conditions – conditions like an Alaskan night.

Could it be that thanks to its large eyes and better-than-average eyesight, the *Troodon* was able to hunt in moonlight, picking off young *Edmontosaurus* as they slumbered in the herd?

It seems that it was the Alaskan *Troodon*'s successful hunting technique that enabled it to thrive and grow to such a large size compared with its southern relations.

NIGHT KILL

1 A herd of edmontosaurs sleeps through the night. The animals huddle close together to conserve heat.

2 Three *Troodon* circle the giants, weighing up whether to attack. Sensing danger the edmontosaurs begin to wake and, one by one, the adults get to their feet to protect their young. Seizing an opportunity, the *Troodon* sprint into the ring, causing panic.

3 A young *Edmontosaurus* makes a fatal error and runs from the protection of the herd. The *Troodons* give chase...

... and attack the infant, slashing at its neck and legs.

4 But help is at hand.

An adult *Edmontosaurus* barges in, knocking the *Troodon* out of the way and bellowing at the hunters.

ALASKA

Be they tyrannosaurids, abelisaurids or freakily large *Troodons*, the new killers of the dinosaur world were vicious opportunists who evolved to ensure that they always won out in the end.

But, as we'll see in the next chapter, sometimes it was their prey that learnt to adapt...

BORN

The Jurassic period saw the first giant dinosaur killers stalking the earth and the seas. Both predator and prey needed to adapt to survive, developing new strategies in the perpetual battle to stay alive. These dinosaurs were born survivors.

SURVIVORS

SEA
MONSTERS

Deep beneath the waves, an ancient angelshark settles on the bottom of the Jurassic ocean. Lying on the seabed, it is completely camouflaged against the sand. Almost immediately it begins to wriggle, churning up clouds of silt around its body. The sand falls gently back to the ocean bed, covering the shark's motionless body. There it will lie, a motionless lump in the sand waiting for prey. It's a tactic that serves the angelshark well. Angelsharks just like this one still exist to this day, and they've hardly changed in 140 million years.

However, this particular angel isn't long for this world.

Behind it, a giant snout ploughs into the sand and rushes towards the shark. Panicked, the angelshark bursts up from its hiding place but is too late. Huge jaws clamp around the creature before it can escape.

PREDATOR X

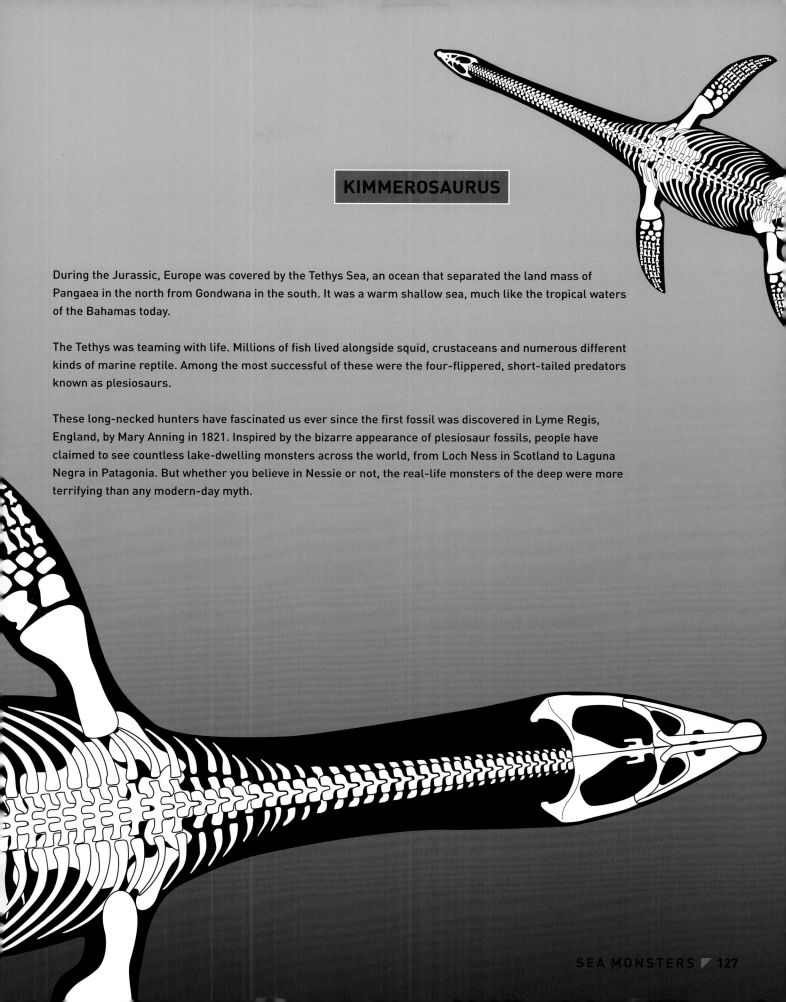

KIMMEROSAURUS

During the Jurassic, Europe was covered by the Tethys Sea, an ocean that separated the land mass of Pangaea in the north from Gondwana in the south. It was a warm shallow sea, much like the tropical waters of the Bahamas today.

The Tethys was teaming with life. Millions of fish lived alongside squid, crustaceans and numerous different kinds of marine reptile. Among the most successful of these were the four-flippered, short-tailed predators known as plesiosaurs.

These long-necked hunters have fascinated us ever since the first fossil was discovered in Lyme Regis, England, by Mary Anning in 1821. Inspired by the bizarre appearance of plesiosaur fossils, people have claimed to see countless lake-dwelling monsters across the world, from Loch Ness in Scotland to Laguna Negra in Patagonia. But whether you believe in Nessie or not, the real-life monsters of the deep were more terrifying than any modern-day myth.

WHAT DID
PLESIOSAURS EAT?

Early palaeontologists believed that plesiosaurs fed exclusively on fish, whipping their long necks around to catch these speedy prey. But a discovery made in 2005 suggested that long-necked plesiosaurs might well have enjoyed a much more varied menu.

This discovery was made by Alex Cook from the Queensland Museum, Colin McHenry from the University of Newcastle and Steve Wroe from the University of Sydney while they were excavating a 6 metre (20 foot) elasmosaurid in Queensland, Australia. Elasmosaurids were especially long-necked plesiosaurs that thrived throughout the Cretaceous. Their necks – in some species about twice as long as the body and tail put together – were the longest necks that have ever evolved.

Like other long-necked plesiosaurs, it was generally thought that elasmosaurids were predators of free-swimming fish and squid, although a restricted amount of flexibility reduced the degree to which the neck could curl or twist. Fossilized fish bones found in the bellies of various North American elasmosaurids supported the idea of a piscivorous diet, and stones have also been discovered in the stomachs of some elasmosaurid species. Perhaps the stones helped the sea monsters control their buoyancy, acting as a kind of ballast that stopped them floating back up to the surface.

A TASTE FOR SHELLFISH

The Queensland elasmosaurid was different. The 110-million year-old stomach region contained bits of broken snail and clamshell. More bits and pieces of shell were preserved in the area occupied in life by the lower intestine, and yet more were found in the part of the skeleton that would originally have housed the creature's bowels. It seems that these remains were the indigestible waste of countless meals. These shell fragments were a puzzle. Elasmosaurid teeth were slim and sharp-tipped, but the jaws probably weren't strong enough to bite through the hard shells of the molluscs the elasmosaurid had been eating.

A STOMACH FULL OF STONES

The answer came in the form of the large polished pebbles, or gastroliths, that were once again found in the stomach. The research team concluded that elasmosaurids like this one fed by swimming close to the seafloor, their incredibly long necks lowered so that the head almost touched the seabed. The animal would then open its mouth and trawl through the silt using its narrowing teeth, swallowing snails, crabs and clams whole. These shelled prey would later have been smashed to pieces by the gastroliths.

More support for this idea was provided by a study of a second elasmosaurid, held in the collections of the Queensland Museum. 135 gastroliths were found in its gut region, some of which had obviously been there a long time before it died. Many were made of volcanic rock that originated over 180 miles from the place where the elasmosaurid eventually died. The creature had been hoovering gastroliths up for years. More importantly, the stomach also contained fragments of crab.

GROOVY CLIFFS

Further evidence for this sort of lifestyle is found in weird grooves preserved in mudrock discovered on a cliff face in Switzerland in the late 1990s. The entire cliff is in fact one giant fossil, an upturned slab of ocean floor from the mid Jurassic. The cliffs are covered in gutters and grooves, some up to 60 cm (24 inches) wide and 9 metres (30 feet) long. These were probably caused by plesiosaurs ploughing their snouts through the sediment at the bottom of the sea in search of worms and molluscs.

COMPETITIVE SEAS

None of this means that elasmosaurids completely avoided free-swimming fish and squid. In fact, it may reveal why elasmosaurids and other long-necked plesiosaurs were so successful for so long. As we've seen with the likes of *Mapusaurus* and *Spinosaurus*, the more you specialize, the more vulnerable you are to changes in your environment. In Jurassic times, plesiosaurs were some of the most successful killers in the sea, but by the Cretaceous they were sharing the water with much larger, fiercer predators, all competing for the same free-swimming fish. Being able to feed from the ocean bed meant the plesiosaurs didn't go hungry. Those impressive, elongated necks were handy multipurpose tools when it came to harvesting food.

GASTROLITHS

A PLESIOSAUR SEA GUTTER

KIMMEROSAURUS LANGHAMI

TRANSLATION
Lizard from Kimmeridge

DIET
Carnivore

HABITAT
European oceans

ERA
Late Jurassic, 147 million years ago

CLASSIFICATION
Plesiosauria, Plesiosauroidea, Cryptoclididae

WEIGHT
1 tonnes (1.1 ton)

LENGTH
6 metres (20 feet)

PADDLES

Long, wing-shaped paddles propelled *Kimmerosaurus* forward at great speeds, thanks to powerful muscles and that strong body. Plesiosaurs flew through the water much like penguins today. The stiff front paddles were used to alter direction while swimming.

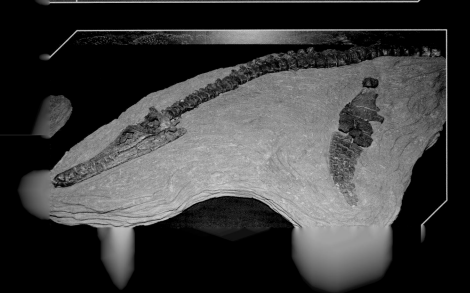

KIM-uhr-o-SORE-uss
LANG-uhm-ie

NECK

Kimmerosaurus had incredibly long necks. Plesiosaur necks contained between 29 and 76 individual vertebrae. Some scientists think that while the long neck helped plesiosaurs catch prey, it may also have slowed them down when swimming.

HEAD

A triangular-shaped head with a wide, flat snout. Up to 72 thin, pointed teeth curved back into its mouth.

BODY

We don't know what a complete *Kimmerosaurus* looked like as only a few vertebrae and a single skull have so far been discovered. In cases like this, palaeontologists make educated guesses by comparing what they know of the animal with the better-preserved remains of close relatives. A rigid backbone, numerous thickened, heavy ribs and enormous, plate-like shoulder and hip bones meant that *Kimmerosaurus*'s broad body was stiff. Plesiosaurs were air-breathing reptiles, meaning that they had to surface regularly to take in oxygen.

TERROR OF THE SEAS

Long-necked plesiosaurs may have been adaptable, but they were by no means the top dogs in the Jurassic seas. In 2006 a monstrous aquatic predator was discovered, one of the most horrifying creatures ever to inhabit the planet's oceans.

The creature was discovered on the Norwegian island of Spitsbergen in the Svalbard archipelago, 1,399 kilometres (800 miles) from the North Pole. A team of palaeontologists led by Jørn Hurum of the University of Oslo was attracted to the island's mountainous region by a number of marine fossils, only to find fragments of a huge pliosaur skull in the permafrost. Pliosaurs were short-necked plesiosaurs, and some of them were very close relatives of such long-necked plesiosaurs as *Kimmerosaurus* and the elasmosaurs. Like long-necked plesiosaurs, pliosaurs hunted fish and squid, but they were also strong enough and big enough to prey on their long-necked cousins as well as other marine reptiles like the shark-shaped ichthyosaurs. They grew to titanic proportions: some reached lengths of up to 11 metres (36 feet). The new Spitsbergen pliosaur was definitely one of the giants – perhaps bigger than any of the kinds discovered beforehand.

Due to the Arctic conditions, Hurum's team only had a short, one-month window on Spitsbergen, extending from the end of July to the end of August. So, the following July they returned to the island and started to unearth a huge trawl of 20,000 fossilized bones. This was difficult, dangerous work, made especially so by the fact that the team had to be constantly on the lookout for curious polar bears.

The reconstructed sea monster they discovered has become known by the nickname it was given by the team. This was –

▶ *PREDATOR X*

PREDATOR X

TRANSLATION	
n/a	
DIET	
Carnivore	
HABITAT	
European oceans	
ERA	
Late Jurassic, 147 million years ago	
CLASSIFICATION	
Plesiosauria, Pliosauroidea	
WEIGHT	
45 tonnes (50 tons)	
LENGTH	
15 metres (49 feet)	

SENSE OF SMELL

Underwater hunters like Predator X relied on a killer sense of smell to track down prey. Studies of pliosaur skulls have revealed internal nostrils set deep into the roofs of their mouths. As they swam, grooves in their maw channelled water to the nostrils where any lingering scents were picked up.

PADDLES

Like all plesiosaurs, Predator X 'flew' through the water propelled by two sets of wing-shaped paddles.

PRED-at-OR EX

BODY

A powerful, muscular, teardrop-shaped body.

SKULL & NECK

Predator X's skull was nearly twice the size of *T. rex*'s. CT scans of pliosaur skulls have shown that these sea monsters had brains roughly the same size and shape as the great white shark's. A short, sturdy neck supported its massive head.

MOUTH & JAWS

Predator X's bone-crushing jaws were 3 metres (10 feet) long. Its teeth were 30 cm (11.8 inches) long, with massive roots that kept them firmly embedded within its jawbones.

ROBO-
PREDATOR

One thing did puzzle the scientists. Predator X seemed to have used all four flippers to swim. That was unlike any living creature. Modern animals such as sea lions and turtles tend only to use one set of flippers to propel themselves forward while steering with the others.

With no living creatures similar to Predator X, the researchers decided they had to create their own. They commissioned John Long of Vassar College, USA, to construct a robot that could mimic Predator X's swimming technique. John Long built Madeleine, a swimming robot roughly the size of a single bed pillow. At first Madeleine was programmed to swim with two flippers and motored along at speed. Then she was programmed to swim with all four. Unsurprisingly she swam faster than before. The downside, however, was that swimming with all four paddles and going at full pelt used far more energy.

This experiment has led some experts to suggest that Predator X swam using just two of its paddles, but used its second pair of flippers when it needed a sudden burst of speed. It's been estimated that, when swimming normally, Predator X could probably reach speeds of 4 metres (13 feet) per second, sprinting at 5 metres (16 feet) per second when using its handy turbo boost. As small plesiosaurs like *Kimmerosaurus* are thought to have reached a maximum swimming speed of only 3 metres (10 feet) per second, any plesiosaur that found itself chased by Predator X would have needed another defence strategy.

PREDATOR X USUALLY SWAM USING ONLY ITS FRONT PADDLES, BUT BY UTILIZING ITS BACK FLIPPERS IT COULD TEAR THROUGH THE WATER AT 5 METRES (16 FEET) PER SECOND.

SHALLOW HAVEN

1 A group of kimmerosaurs chase fish in the open sea. But they are being watched by Predator X, lurking nearby. Spotting the danger, the school of kimmerosaurs make a break for it.

Predator X gives chase.

2 Metre by metre, it gains on the smaller *Kimmerosaurus* at the back of the group, its crocodile-like jaws ready to strike. The *Kimmerosaurus*'s only hope is to reach the sanctuary of shallow water.

3 The *Kimmerosaurus* makes it into shallow water where Predator X can't follow, its sheer bulk working against it.

SAFE
AND SOUND

The ability to use shallow waters as a refuge might perhaps have been the difference between life and death for plesiosaurs. And in 2005 a discovery made on a remote Antarctic Island revealed that it was probably also a strategy the creatures used to protect their vulnerable young.

MAUISAURUS FOSSIL, VEGA ISLAND

A team of palaeontologists led by James E. Martin, of the South Dakota School of Mines and Technology's Museum of Geology, Judd Case of Eastern Washington University and Marcelo Reguero of Museo de La Plata, Argentina braved 113 kph (70 mph) Antarctic winds to uncover a baby plesiosaur identified as a *Mauisaurus*. The near-complete elasmosaurid skeleton, discovered in the Sandwich Bluff area of Vega Island, was 1.5 metres (5 feet) long and came from rocks dated to the Late Cretaceous. If it had survived to adulthood, the baby would have grown to over 8 metres (26 feet) in length.

The fact that it was found surrounded by fossils of marine invertebrates seemed to suggest that it died in especially shallow water. And it wasn't alone. Other, as yet unidentified, juvenile fossils were found too. Perhaps this lagoon was a nursery, a protected area where plesiosaurs came to give birth to their babies. It seems reasonable to assume that the young remained in the safety of the shallows until they grew large enough to face the perils of the open sea.

Unfortunately for this *Mauisaurus*, the area was covered in a layer of volcanic ash. While the nursery was a safe haven from killers such as Predator X, the young couldn't be protected from a volcanic eruption.

Young plesiosaurs couldn't languish in lagoons for ever. Eventually they would have to venture into deeper water and, out there, the possibility of a volcano was the least of their worries.

Fossils of plesiosaurs are common all around the world, as are the bite marks – deep gashes into the bones themselves – found on them. Some sea reptiles appear to survived these injuries, but others weren't so lucky. Plenty of skeletons were disarticulated, ripped apart by other, larger predators.

One particular fossil tells a chilling story. In 1981 an *Eromangasaurus* skull was excavated from the Toolebuc Formation of Yambore Creek in central northern Queensland, Australia. Severely crushed, the skull was only connected to five vertebrae.

IT WAS MISSING ITS BODY

When the fossil was examined, the cause of death became clear. The eromangasaur seems to have been killed after suffering a devastating bite from a large pliosaur, a bite that severed the head from the rest of its body. The angle of the damage indicates that the attack came from below, perhaps showing that – like great white sharks today – giant pliosaurs like Predator X rushed up from below when attacking prey.

All of these fossils were preserved in sediments once deposited in deep water: the sort of environment where plesiosaurs would forage and feed, but also that in which they were in the most danger.

OFF WITH ITS HEAD

1 A *Kimmerosaurus* basks just under the surface of the water, taking welcome gulps of air from above. Deep below, Predator X picks up the scent of the lone kimmerosaur.

2 Unaware of the danger, the long-necked plesiosaur hunts near the surface... and Predator X strikes, powering upwards using all four of its paddles. It crashes into the *Kimmerosaurus*, knocking the air out of its lungs.

3 Stunned, the *Kimmerosaurus* struggles to escape. Predator X attacks again, ripping away one of the plesiosaur's rear paddles.

4 Losing blood fast, *Kimmerosaurus* makes for the sanctuary of a nearby lagoon, but Predator X dives, zooming under the stricken reptile. It shoots up again, opening its maw...

5 ... and bursts out of the ocean, the kimmerosaur trapped helpless in the predator's tremendous jaws...

6 The kimmerosaur's neck is severed in mere seconds, and Predator X grabs the decapitated body in triumph.

THE REAL
JAWS

Predator X's bite was formidable. It's estimated that the pliosaur could bite down with a force of 15 tonnes (16.5 tons) – far greater than any creature currently living on Earth and four times as powerful as *Tyrannosaurus rex*. Scientists estimate that this would be enough to crush a 4x4 vehicle.

Crushing down hard, its 30 cm (12 inch) teeth could perforate the body of its victim, slicing through muscle and bone. After which it would thrash the body back and forth in the water, shaking the corpse to pieces.

EUROPE

MORRISON MONSTERS

Pliosaurs ruled the oceans for 70 million years; buoyed by the water, and able to exploit a rich variety of large prey animals, they evolved into giants. Of course, the oceans weren't the only places where giant, Mesozoic reptiles evolved.

The 1870s were an exciting time for dinosaur discoveries in North America. The Morrison Formation, a 1,554,000 square kilometre (600,000 square mile) area of late Jurassic rock in Colorado, USA, was searched extensively for dinosaur bones. Every year seemed to bring new finds – discoveries that would shape what we know about dinosaurs today.

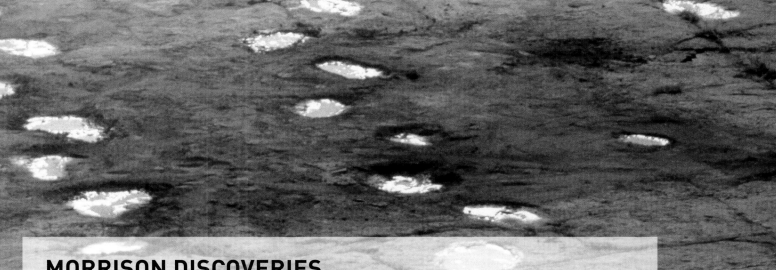

MORRISON DISCOVERIES

Many of the most famous dinosaurs were discovered in the Morrison Formation in the late 1870s:

1877   Palaeontologist Othniel Charles Marsh names *Stegosaurus armatus* from remains found in the Morrison Formation.

1877   Marsh's bone-hunting rival Edward Drinker Cope names *Camarasaurus* from a few scattered vertebrae.

1877   *Allosaurus fragilis* is named by Marsh.

1878   *Diplodocus longus* is described by Marsh, based on a skeleton discovered at Cañon City by Benjamin Mudge and Samuel Wendell Williston the previous year.

1879   Marsh names *Brontosaurus excelsus* from remains found in Wyoming (this species would later be renamed *Apatosaurus ajax*).

One of the most formidable carnivores of Jurassic North America was –

▶ *ALLOSAURUS,*

a 1.7 tonne (1.9 ton) killer that dominated the area for at least 20 million years.

We perhaps know more about this theropod than any other Mesozoic dinosaur, largely due to the fact that they were so successful and so many *Allosaurus* skeletons have been found. One particular site, the Cleveland-Lloyd Quarry of Utah, has yielded approximately 46 individual *Allosaurus* skeletons since 1927.

ALLOSAURUS

ALLOSAURUS FRAGILIS

TRANSLATION
Fragile different lizard

DIET
Carnivore

HABITAT
Colorado, Utah, USA

ERA
Late Jurassic, 155–145 million years ago

CLASSIFICATION
Saurischia, Theropoda, Allosauroidea

WEIGHT
2.3 tonnes (2.5 tons)

LENGTH
8.5–10 metres (28–33 feet)

BODY

With so many allosaur fossils, we can estimate that *Allosaurus* reached its full adult size by the age of 15. Barring accidents or attacks, it's likely it could have lived for another 10 to 15 years. *Allosaurus* was named after its vertebrae which, at the time, were different from those of any dinosaur yet found. They appeared more delicately built than the vertebrae of previous discoveries, although time would show that vertebrae of this shape and form were actually quite common. The *fragilis* part of the name came from Marsh's belief that the vertebrae would have lacked strength.

LEGS

Allosaurus's legs were shorter than those of the great Cretaceous tyrannosaurids and not suited for speed. This suggests that *Allosaurus* was an ambush killer.

PRONUNCIATION

Al-oh-SORE-uss
fra-jill-uss

HORNS

While the horns above *Allosaurus*'s eyes may have given it an intimidating appearance, it's unlikely that they were used as weapons. It's more likely that they were used to attract potential mates.

HEAD & NECK

A short, muscular, S-shaped neck supported *Allosaurus*'s massive head. Its serrated teeth averaged about 10 cm (4 inches) in length. *Allosaurus* constantly grew new teeth inside its jaws, ready to replace any older ones lost while fighting or eating. The part of its brain that processed smells was quite large, meaning that it probably used a keen sense of smell while hunting. *Allosaurus* could hear low frequencies but would have had trouble picking up more subtle sounds.

ARMS

Allosaurus could use its short, strong arms to grab its victims. Its three-fingered hands ended in vicious claws that could grow to lengths of 25 cm (10 inches). Shaped like eagles' claws, they could have enabled it to latch on to prey animals.

MYSTERIOUS KILLER

ALLOSAURUS
TOOTH

Allosaurus may have been one of the more ferocious killers of the Late Jurassic, but various aspects of its biology and behaviour are a bit of a mystery. Its teeth are fairly short for its size and its jawbone is surprisingly narrow. We know from preserved bite marks that allosaurs were formidable, successful predators, but how exactly did they kill their prey? Surely teeth and jaws like this would have struggled to chomp through bone and muscle?

BIG AL'S WEAK BITE

The answer was revealed by a study of Big Al, a near-complete *Allosaurus* skeleton found in Wyoming in 1991. Studies of Big Al's bones revealed that the dinosaur didn't have an easy life. Its skeleton shows signs of numerous breaks and even bacterial infections; these problems perhaps brought about the animal's premature death. But Emily Rayfield of the University of Cambridge wasn't interested in what killed this particular allosaur. Instead she was mostly interested in how its skull and jaw worked.

Working with researchers from Canada and the USA, Rayfield created a three-dimensional model of Big Al's skull – the most complicated virtual model of a dinosaur ever attempted. Comparing Big Al's skull to that of a cow helped Rayfield's team estimate how much muscle would have been connected to the bones and just how strong they would have been. Finally they turned to a process called Finite Element Analysis that is used in engineering to work out how much stress a bridge can take before breaking.

The tests revealed two things about Big Al's head:

1. WEAK BITE

Big Al's jaws were even weaker than had been imagined. The strongest bite force it could muster was a paltry 200 kg (441 lb), a fraction of that of *Tyrannosaurus rex* or even some alligators today. It was roughly the equivalent of a leopard. There was no way that Big Al's jaws could have shattered bones.

2. STRONG SKULL

That didn't mean that Big Al's skull was in any way feeble. Yes, his bite was surprisingly puny, but his skull was extremely good at transmitting force along its length. It had more openings and was considerably lighter than the skull of *T. rex*, but was structured in such a way that it could withstand amazing levels of stress. The Finite Element Analysis showed that the skull could take an impact equivalent to 6 tonnes (6.6 tons) before breaking.

The implication is that *Allosaurus* used its head like a hatchet, using strong neck muscles to ram the teeth of its upper jaw into the body of its prey. Every impact would tear the allosaur's serrated teeth though its victim's flesh. Prey animals would have included such plant eaters as *Camptosaurus*, *Stegosaurus* and juvenile sauropods.

HATCHET KILLER

1

A lone *Camptosaurus* grazes on the plain, unaware that it is being watched by a ravenous *Allosaurus*.

A fast and powerful ambush hunter, *Allosaurus* suddenly tears forwards. The *Camptosaurus* flees, hoping to outrun the two-tonne killer. Running alongside its prey, the *Allosaurus* swats the smaller herbivore off its feet.

2

The *Allosaurus* opens its mouth and slams its dagger-like fangs deep into the *Camptosaurus*'s back. Blow after blow, the relentless attack continues until the *Camptosaurus* collapses from shock and blood loss. The kill isn't pretty. It isn't even clinical, but it is ruthlessly efficient.

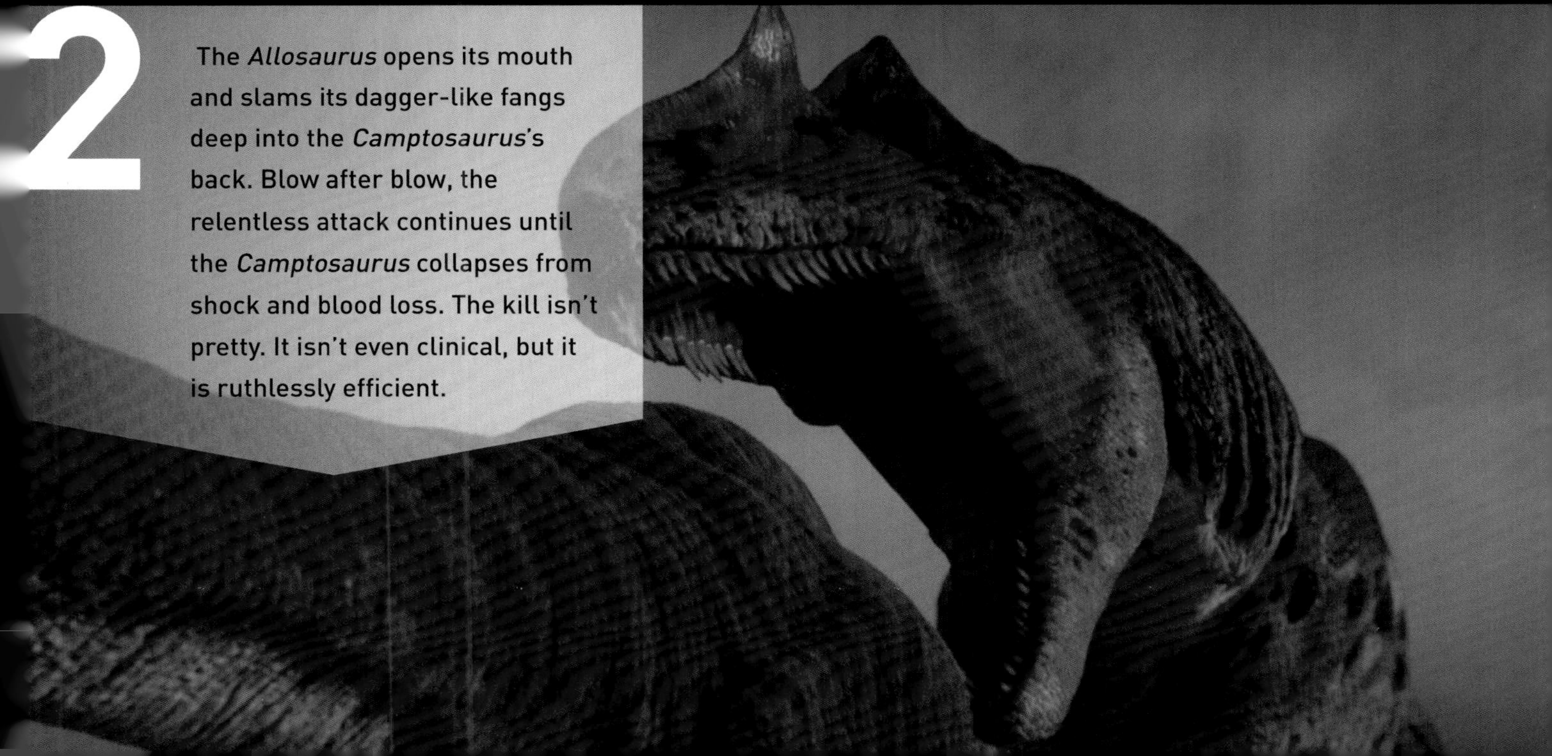

NORTH AMERICA

CAMPTOSAURUS

TRANSLATION
Flexible lizard

DIET
Herbivore

HABITAT
Colorado, Utah, USA

ERA
Late Jurassic, 147 million years ago

CLASSIFICATION
Ornithischia, Ornithopoda, Iguanodontia,
Camptosauridae

WEIGHT
500 kg (1,100 lbs)

LENGTH
5 metres (16 feet)

BODY

A large, deep body housed huge guts. A series of tendons criss-crossed alongside the backbone to make the spine stronger and kept *Camptosaurus*'s back stiff.

DISCOVERY

In 1879, Othniel Charles Marsh described an ornithopod discovered earlier that same year by William Harlow Reed in Albany County, New York, USA. It was named *Camptonotus* or 'flexible back', as the vertebrae located between the two halves of the hip girdle (known as the sacral vertebrae) seemed not to be fused together. Unfortunately, the name had already been used for a cricket, so in 1885 *Camptonotus* was renamed *Camptosaurus*, meaning 'flexible lizard'. Either way, the name eventually proved inaccurate as subsequent fossils confirmed that *Camptosaurus* had fused sacral vertebrae.

kamp-toe-SORE-uss

HEAD

Camptosaurus's skull was almost horse-like in appearance. A peculiar bone known as the palpebral grew over the eye socket. We don't know what purpose this served.

BEAK

Broad-beaked lower and upper jaws tore through tougher vegetation. Mobile joints let the cheeks move in and out so that *Camptosaurus*'s leaf-shaped teeth could grind against each other to mash up food.

LIMBS

Stocky forearms could easily have supported *Camptosaurus*'s weight. While it probably stood on two legs to reach high vegetation or run, we think *Camptosaurus* sometimes walked on all fours. Several of the wrist bones were fused together for strength to support the camptosaur's 500 kg (1,100 lb) weight. Its fingers were splayed out rather than bound together in a pad, like those of *Iguanodon*. Three of its fingers ended in small hooves. *Camptosaurus* had massive toe bones. The first toe was shorter than the others and wouldn't have reached the ground.

SAFETY IN NUMBERS

On its own, *Camptosaurus* could never have stood up to the might of *Allosaurus*. Perhaps, some suggest, this is why it took to living alongside heavy-duty friends; namely, the flamboyant, spiky-tailed herbivore known as

▶ *STEGOSAURUS*

TWO BRAINS BETTER THAN ONE?

A large cavity located within the vertebrae of the hip region once led some palaeontologists to suggest that *Stegosaurus* possessed a sort of 'second brain' that perhaps helped control the rear of its massive body. Actually, a cavity of the same sort is common in modern birds and is nothing to do with brain power. It houses a structure called the glycogen body. This might function as an energy store, but a role in balance has also been suggested.

COMRADES IN ARMS

It seems plausible that these two types of herbivore stuck close together. Why? Perhaps because their particular talents and tastes perfectly complemented each other, offering mutual protection in a world where danger lurked around every corner.

Even though both species were herbivores, they almost certainly exploited different kinds of vegetation. *Stegosaurus*'s narrow muzzle was suited for a diet of small, relatively soft objects. Computer analysis suggests that it had an incredibly weak bite and would have struggled to chew through a twig more than a centimetre (0.4 inches) in diameter. *Camptosaurus*, with teeth four times bigger than *Stegosaurus*'s, could chop up much tougher vegetation. It's likely that the larger *Stegosaurus* would muscle *Camptosaurus* out of the way to get to the freshest vegetation, leaving *Camptosaurus* to nip in and rifle through what was left. And if the pickings got slim, *Stegosaurus* could rear up on its hind legs to reach the lush, new growth of conifers several metres above ground level, well beyond the reach of *Camptosaurus*.

From studying stegosaur brain cases, we know that the plate-backed beasts had an acute sense of smell. *Camptosaurus*, on the other hand, had much better eyesight. If these herbivores had worked together, they would have had a better chance of detecting danger, such as a surprise ambush by *Allosaurus*. The keen-eyed *Camptosaurus* could have provided an early-warning system, whereas the armoured *Stegosaurus* might have been the obvious, brightly coloured deterrent.

STEGOSAURUS

CAMPTOSAURUS

BEST OF FRIENDS?

Fossils of *Stegosaurus* and *Camptosaurus* have occasionally been found together. However, one discovery suggests that the two dinosaurs might perhaps have enjoyed a particularly close relationship. Fossil footprints, discovered in Morrison Formation rocks, showed individuals of these two species walking along, side by side.

STEGOSAURUS

TRANSLATION
Roof lizard

DIET
Herbivore

HABITAT
North America and Western Europe

ERA
Late Jurassic,156–140 million years ago

CLASSIFICATION
Ornithischia, Thyreophora, Stegosauria, Stegosauridae

WEIGHT
2.7 tonnes (2.73 tons)

LENGTH
8.5 metres (28 feet)

PLATE POWER

Did *Stegosaurus*'s plates protect it from attack? Probably not. Because they were made of thin, spongey bone and were full of blood vessels, a popular idea has been that they functioned in temperature control. If *Stegosaurus* turned sideways towards the sun, they could have absorbed heat, while they could have dissipated heat when turned towards a breeze. Another idea is that the plates were all for show, to attract mates.

DISCOVERY

The first *Stegosaurus* remains were discovered in western North America in 1877 by Arthur Lakes, and were named and described by Othniel Charles Marsh. In 2006, *Stegosaurus* fossils were found near the city of Batalha, Portugal, meaning this dinosaur was more widespread than previously thought. Some experts think that Chinese stegosaur fossils should also be identified as belonging to *Stegosaurus*, in which case it truly was a transcontinental dinosaur.

FEET

Hoof-like nails tipped at least some of the fingers on the five-toed forefeet. Broad hind feet, complete with three blunt toes, supported *Stegosaurus*'s immense weight.

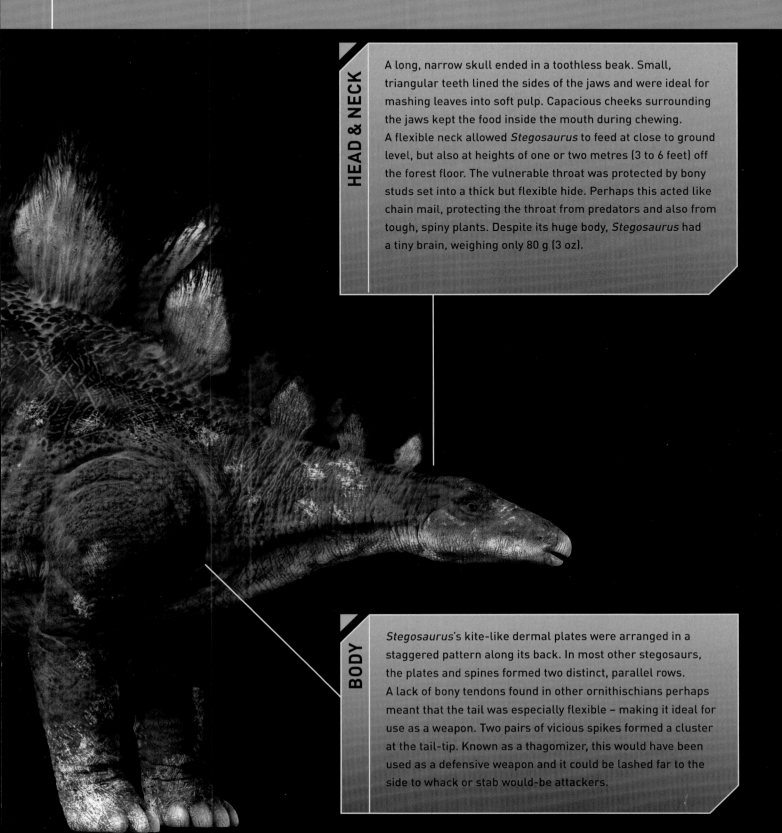

HEAD & NECK

A long, narrow skull ended in a toothless beak. Small, triangular teeth lined the sides of the jaws and were ideal for mashing leaves into soft pulp. Capacious cheeks surrounding the jaws kept the food inside the mouth during chewing. A flexible neck allowed *Stegosaurus* to feed at close to ground level, but also at heights of one or two metres (3 to 6 feet) off the forest floor. The vulnerable throat was protected by bony studs set into a thick but flexible hide. Perhaps this acted like chain mail, protecting the throat from predators and also from tough, spiny plants. Despite its huge body, *Stegosaurus* had a tiny brain, weighing only 80 g (3 oz).

BODY

Stegosaurus's kite-like dermal plates were arranged in a staggered pattern along its back. In most other stegosaurs, the plates and spines formed two distinct, parallel rows. A lack of bony tendons found in other ornithischians perhaps meant that the tail was especially flexible – making it ideal for use as a weapon. Two pairs of vicious spikes formed a cluster at the tail-tip. Known as a thagomizer, this would have been used as a defensive weapon and it could be lashed far to the side to whack or stab would-be attackers.

TWO HEADS
ARE BETTER THAN ONE

1 A herd of stegosaurs graze alongside their ever-present *Camptosaurus* companions. One of the *Camptosaurus* rears up. It has spotted something hiding behind the huge termite-mounds that dot the landscape. It is an *Allosaurus*. The *Camptosaurus* cries out a warning...

2 ... and the herd flees, leaving the starving ambush predator facing a *Stegosaurus*'s vicious thagomizer.

3

The stegosaur is virtually impregnable from behind, meaning that the allosaur has to try and attack the herbivore from the front.

4

The *Allosaurus* strikes, driving its teeth down onto the narrow head of a *Stegosaurus*...

5

... only to be rewarded by a hefty thwack of a thagomizer into its side. The metre-long spikes collide with the allosaur's body, stabbing so deep that one punches clean through its spine.

The ponderous stegosaurs trudge away, leaving the fallen theropod roaring in pain and losing blood fast.

BATTLING GIANTS

Extraordinary evidence proves that stegosaurs and allosaurs sometimes clashed in deadly battles. In 2005, a *Stegosaurus* plate was unearthed with a U-shaped bite mark – a bite mark that perfectly matched the jaws of an *Allosaurus*.

That's not all. Experts have also found an *Allosaurus* tail vertebra that shows evidence of impact with a thagomizer strike. The spikes had been travelling so fast that they'd punched a hole right through one of the allosaur's vertebrae. Amazingly, the bone had started to repair – proof that the allosaur survived the attack.

THE ALLOSAURUS GRAVEYARD

The Cleveland-Lloyd Quarry in Utah is unusual because it has yielded so many *Allosaurus* skeletons. Just how did so many allosaurs end up dying in the same location, especially when just 10 per cent or so of the dinosaur population of Earth at that time is thought to have been made up of predators? There are two main hypotheses:

1. DEATH BY BOG
During the Late Jurassic, an area close to the quarry was occupied by a massive lake. It seems that its banks were formed by layers of thick, sticky mud. This trapped the dinosaurs that waded out to the water for a drink. Perhaps the opportunistic allosaurs were attracted to the pitiful cries of these unfortunate, mired herbivores, and then got trapped themselves after walking out to feast on these easy prey. More and more bodies built up over time, the stench of their rotting bodies attracting ever more predators to the site. Locations that lure in predators like this are known as predator traps.

2. DEATH BY DROUGHT
In 2002, Terry Gates of the University of Utah, USA, suggested an alternative interpretation. Gates had tried and failed to find a modern predator trap where the predators had repeatedly become trapped by miring, and he was left wondering whether such a huge number of allosaurs could possibly have met their ends in this way.

Gates studied the numerous allosaur fossils from Utah, but could find none of the expected signs that the dinosaurs had died following miring. You'd expect such bones to remain articulated, since the skeletons of animals that die while mired tend to remain in their original positions. Yet none of the Utah allosaur bones were articulated. Furthermore, their leg bones should have been preserved vertically, since mired animals generally die in a standing position. Again, there's no evidence of this in the quarry. What Gates did find were indications that the area had suffered from a severe drought, such as preserved cracks in the mud.

Then there's the fact that 82 per cent of the *Allosaurus* remains found in the quarry represent young individuals. As juvenile animals are particularly susceptible to extreme environmental changes, Gates argued that their premature deaths were consistent with an exceptionally harsh drought. Parched and desperate for water, the herbivores of the area would have made for the lake, only to find it dried up. Congregating at the few remaining watering holes, the plant eaters would have stripped the remaining vegetation and died of hunger. The allosaurs would have descended on the carcasses – the only ones available for miles – only to face a long, lingering death from starvation, dehydration, disease and heatstroke when the bodies had run out.

Whatever fate befell them, the multiple deaths of the Cleveland-Lloyd allosaurs prove that, no matter how fierce a hunter you are, your days are numbered when your prey adapts to defend itself – or disappears entirely.

Over the last decade, China has become the vanguard of the new dinosaur revolution. Some of the most unusal dinosaurs ever seen have been discovered, giving us a glimpse of an alien world and painting a compelling picture of the evolution and development of feathers. This is where the dinosaurs took flight.

TAKING FLIGHT

FIRST FEATHERS

ARCHAEOPTERYX

If you take a look out of your window right now, the chances are that you will see a dinosaur hopping about. The idea that birds evolved from dinosaurs is nothing new. In 1870, English biologist Thomas Henry Huxley drew attention to strong similarities present between the leg of an ostrich and the hind limbs of the dinosaurs *Hypsilophodon* and *Compsognathus*. In 1877, Othniel Marsh specifically suggested that birds had evolved from among the dinosaurs, and this view soon became popular.

Eight years previously, the fossilized remains of *Archaeopteryx*, the earliest known bird, had been unearthed in Bavaria. Today, *Archaeopteryx* is of utmost importance in our interpretation of early bird evolution, but its significance was debated during the 1800s. Here was a creature that had feathers and was probably capable of flight, yet it also had sharp teeth, clawed hands and a bony tail, much like a small carnivorous dinosaur.

It would take nearly 100 years for Huxley's link between birds and dinosaurs to be accepted by the majority of the scientific community. In the 1970s, American palaeontologist John Ostrom published several scientific articles in which he argued that Huxley and Marsh had been right. New information allowed Ostrom to show that carnivorous dinosaurs like *Deinonychus* were extremely similar to *Archaeopteryx*. *Deinonychus* was a swift, deadly hunter with intriguingly bird-like qualities to its wrist, shoulder and skull. Ostrom's proposal was detailed and insightful, and he immediately convinced many – though not all – of his colleagues that birds were, indeed, the direct descendants of *Deinonychus*-like theropods. Today, the idea that dinosaurs live on as birds is widely accepted. As we'll see, a large number of spectacularly preserved fossil theropods have provided strong support for Ostrom's argument.

FEATHERED DINOSAURS

In 1996, a 90 cm (36 inch) dinosaur fossil was discovered in the Liaoning province in north-eastern China. Perfectly preserved on a slab of silt stone and volcanic ash, *Sinosauropteryx* showed traces of primitive feathers down its spine and along its sides. The feathers themselves were no more than a fuzzy down, too short to allow the dinosaur to fly and more likely intended to keep it warm. Whatever their role, this was a groundbreaking discovery and one that would change the way we would view dinosaurs for ever.

CLIMBING WINGS

Suddenly, Liaoning's Cretaceous-age Yixian Formation became one of the most important fossil locations on the planet. Today it has revealed more feathered dinosaurs than we ever thought possible. The first decade of the 21st century saw dozens of discoveries that strengthened the link between birds and other theropods. In 2008, the earliest and possibly most bizarre feathered dinosaur was presented to the world. Belonging to a family known as the scansoriopterygids or 'climbing wings', *Epidexipteryx* was a pigeon-sized predator that liked to show off.

▶ *EPIDEXIPTERYX*

CHINA

The fossil was first described in 2008 by a team led by Fucheng Zhang of the Chinese Academy of Science. It had originally been discovered a year before, in Nincheng County, Inner Mongolia, in the Daohugou Formation. The geological age of these rock beds has always been controversial. Some say that the fossils found here are from the Early Cretaceous while others place them as far back as the Middle Jurassic. If the latter is true, it means that *Epidexipteryx* was strutting its stuff a few million years before *Archaeopteryx* evolved.

And strut it did. There was no way that its fuzzy body feathers could have provided enough lift to get *Epidexipteryx* off the ground. Then there are those two sets of tail feathers. Again, they would be useless when it came to flying and would offer nothing in the way of insulation. Highly conspicuous, they are so out of proportion that they would often have got in the way when scurrying around the forest floor.

The only logical conclusion is that they were there to be seen. Like peacocks today, the purely ornamental tail feathers had seemingly evolved to stand out and attract potential mates. We can't tell whether the fossil remains are male or female, but if *Epidexipteryx* is anything like modern birds, it was probably the male of the species that made a spectacle of itself – advertising its good genes through extraordinary plumage. This incredible find proves that feathers were used to attract mates long before they were ever used to take to the wing.

EPIDEXIPTERYX HUI

TRANSLATION
Hu's display feather

DIET
Carnivore or insectivore

HABITAT
Mongolia, China

ERA
Mid to Late Jurassic, 168–152 million years ago

CLASSIFICATION
Saurischia, Theropoda, Coelurosauria,
Maniraptora, Scansoriopterygidae

WEIGHT
160 g (5.5 oz)

LENGTH
30 cm (1 foot)

FEATHERS

Four ribbon-like feathers sprouted from the end of
Epidexipteryx's tail. As the tips of the fossil's tail feathers have
broken off we have no way of knowing how long they actually
were, but it's likely they stretched to at least 20 cm (8 inches).
Short, fuzzy feathers covered its shoulders and body.

FEET

Epidexipteryx had claws similar in shape to those of ground-
foraging birds such as turkeys.

Epi-decks-ip-ter-icks hwee

HEAD

Nostrils were positioned high on *Epidexipteryx*'s snout. Its sharp front teeth pointed outward, making them ideal for grabbing small mammals, insects or reptiles.

ARMS

Epidexipteryx had long arms and hands. An elongated third finger, found in all scansoriopterygids, was perhaps used to dig out beetle grubs from wood. The feathers were too short to support the dinosaur in flight, so it perhaps scurried on the ground and also clambered about among branches.

NEST
RAIDERS

A troodontid known as *Saurornithoides mongoliensis* (Mongolian bird lizard) has built a shallow nest out of dirt and sand, a nest that will eventually contain up to 24 tightly packed eggs. Desperate for food, the troodontid covers the nest with leaves and heads off to scavenge. But its departure has been noted. An oviraptorosaur approaches the unguarded nest. But surely a theropod with no teeth has to be a plant eater?

Surely the eggs are safe?

AN EASY MEAL?

Of course, feathers aren't the only feature that Jurassic and Cretaceous theropods like *Epidexipteryx* share with modern birds. As we've seen, they often laid their eggs in nests. And wherever there are nests, there are predators looking for a quick snack.

One of these predators was –

▶ *OVIRAPTOR*

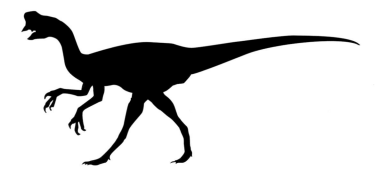

MEAT OR VEG?

So did *Oviraptor* eat plants or meat? Let's consider the evidence:

EVIDENCE THAT OVIRAPTOR WAS A HERBIVORE:

– It seems that *Oviraptor*'s lower jaw was able to slide back and forth, a feature often seen in herbivorous animals. Was this ability present so that *Oviraptor* could slice though tough vegetation?

– Some oviraptorosaur skeletons contain gastroliths – stones swallowed to help break down vegetable matter in the stomach.

EVIDENCE THAT OVIRAPTOR WAS A CARNIVORE:

– The bones of a small lizard were found near the stomach cavity of the original *Oviraptor* skeleton, discovered in 1923.

– In 1993, a nest containing oviraptorosaur eggs was found at Ukhaa Tolgod, Mongolia. But they weren't alone. Two small skulls covered with eggshell scraps were also discovered in the nest – but these skulls possessed teeth. They didn't belong to an oviraptorosaur. They were probably troodontid skulls.

HOW DID THE TROODONTIDS END UP IN AN OVIRAPTORID NEST?

There are three possibilities:

1. The troodontid species concerned was a nest parasite. It muscled into other dinosaurs' nests to lay its eggs, like the modern cuckoo (and the cuckoo is far from unique: nest parasitism is widespread in birds).

2. The troodontids were feeding on the oviraptorosaur eggs. This is unlikely. The troodontid skulls are from tiny babies that were probably too young to mount an attack on another nest.

3. The oviraptorosaur parent snatched troodontid eggs or hatchings to feed its own young.

This third option is the most likely explanation. *Oviraptor* and related oviraptorosaurs were probably adapted to eat both flesh and plant life, feasting on the eggs of other dinosaurs on occasion. This made them flexible, adaptable animals able to survive successfully virtually anywhere.

OVIRAPTOR
PHILOCERATOPS

TRANSLATION
Egg-stealer, with a taste for a ceratopsian egg

DIET
Omnivore

HABITAT
Mongolian desert dunes

ERA
Late Cretaceous, 75 million years ago

CLASSIFICATION
Saurischia, Theropoda, Coelurosauria,

Maniraptora, Oviraptorosauria

WEIGHT
22 kg (50 lb)

LENGTH
2.1 metres (7 feet)

BODY
In many ways the *Oviraptor* skeleton resembles that of a modern flightless bird. Downy feathers covered its body.

oh-vir-rap-TOR
phil-oh-sera-tops

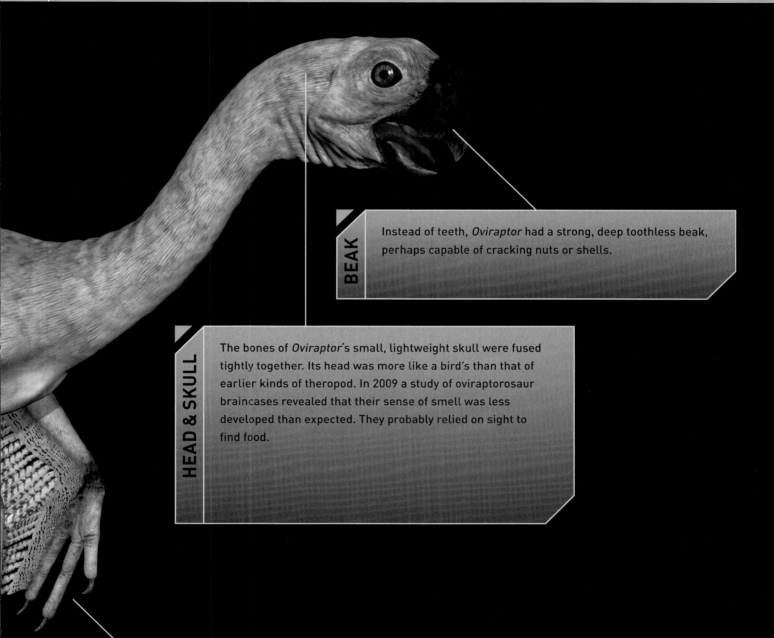

BEAK

Instead of teeth, *Oviraptor* had a strong, deep toothless beak, perhaps capable of cracking nuts or shells.

HEAD & SKULL

The bones of *Oviraptor*'s small, lightweight skull were fused tightly together. Its head was more like a bird's than that of earlier kinds of theropod. In 2009 a study of oviraptorosaur braincases revealed that their sense of smell was less developed than expected. They probably relied on sight to find food.

HANDS

Long, grabbing, three-fingered hands armed with needle-sharp, curved claws.

A NASTY SURPRISE

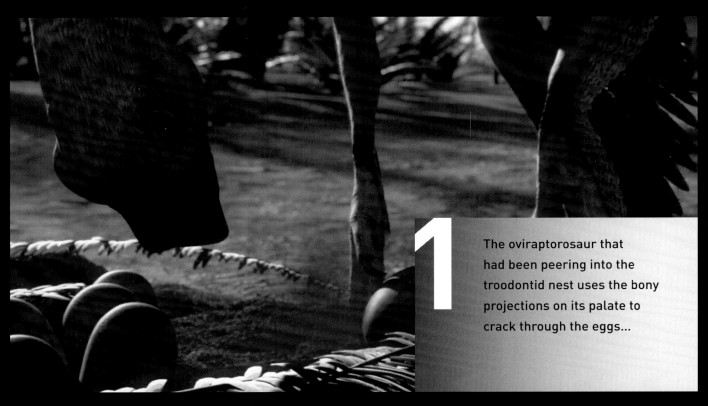

1 The oviraptorosaur that had been peering into the troodontid nest uses the bony projections on its palate to crack through the eggs...

2 ... until it is disturbed by the hasty return of the troodontid parent.

3

The oviraptorosaur flees the scene of the crime. But two lost eggs are the least of the troodontid parent's problems. A massive beak plunges down from the sky and plucks the shocked theropod into the air, slamming it back into the ground to break its spine.

Not all oviraptorosaurs in Cretaceous Mongolia were small fry.

This is –

▶ *GIGANTORAPTOR*

GIGANTORAPTOR ERLIANENSIS

TRANSLATION
Giant thief from Erlian (a city in Inner Mongolia)

DIET
Unknown (but probably omnivorous)

HABITAT
The woodlands of northern China

ERA
Late Cretaceous, 80 million years ago

CLASSIFICATION
Saurischia, Theropoda, Coelurosauria,
Maniraptora, Oviraptorosauria

WEIGHT
2.4–2.6 tonnes (2.6–2.9 tons)

LENGTH
8 metres (26 feet)

DISCOVERY

The *Gigantoraptor* remains were found by complete accident by Xu Xing of the
Institute of Vertebrate Paleontology and Paleoanthropology (IVPP) in Beijing. In
April 2005, Xu was re-enacting the discovery of sauropod bones for a Japanese
television documentary. The cameras started rolling as the palaeontologist
plucked a random bone from the site of his dig. Immediately, Xu realised that
he didn't have a sauropod bone in his hand. Was it a tyrannosaur? It was certainly
big enough. Xu turned to the director and ordered him to turn off the cameras –
he didn't want this unexpected discovery broadcast to the entire world.

Xu's team set to work and eventually excavated a largely complete skeleton,
including a lower jaw, fore and hind limbs, vertebrae and a partial pelvis.

To see how old their discovery was when it died, the scientists sliced through one
of the *Gigantoraptor*'s leg bones. They estimated it was 11 years old at the time of
death and was probably still growing. A full adult would have been even bigger.

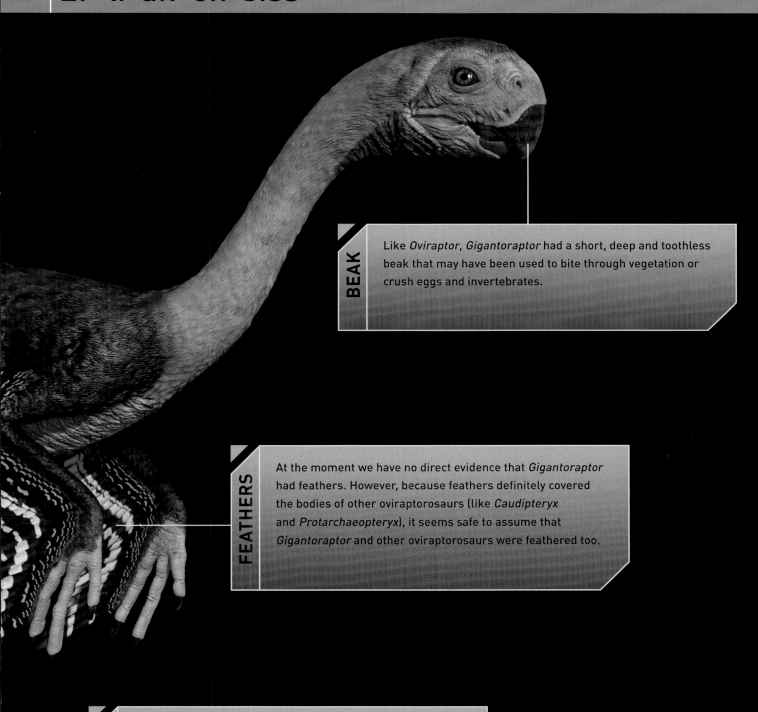

BEAK

Like *Oviraptor*, *Gigantoraptor* had a short, deep and toothless beak that may have been used to bite through vegetation or crush eggs and invertebrates.

FEATHERS

At the moment we have no direct evidence that *Gigantoraptor* had feathers. However, because feathers definitely covered the bodies of other oviraptorosaurs (like *Caudipteryx* and *Protarchaeopteryx*), it seems safe to assume that *Gigantoraptor* and other oviraptorosaurs were feathered too.

LEGS

Long, slender legs

Despite its feathers, *Gigantoraptor* was obviously not capable of flight. Perhaps its feathering helped shield it from the heat of the sun, or kept it warm during cool nights. It's also possible that, as with the tiny *Epidexipteryx*, these feathers partly functioned in display – making *Gigantoraptor* appear more threatening or improving its chances in attracting a mate.

But this wasn't the case for all dinosaurs. In the late 1990s a dromaeosaur was discovered with feathers that looked exactly the same as those found on modern birds. Was this finally a dinosaur that could fly?

GIGANTORAPTOR'S DISPLAY FEATHERS WERE USED FOR BOTH FIGHTING AND FOR FINDING A MATE.

MONGOLIA

TREETOP TUSSLE

1 The sun sets on the forest, its last rays breaking through the canopy of trees. All around, the nocturnal inhabitants of the treetop world are waking. A lone lizard, *Xianglong zhaoi*, scampers up a gnarled tree trunk, looking for food. It darts this way and that in the fading light, stopping to pounce on an unsuspecting insect.

But here, the hunter must be wary at all times. The *Xianglong* hasn't noticed a huddle of perfectly camouflaged feathers pressed against the bark further up the tree. It hasn't noticed the sharp eyes peering down.

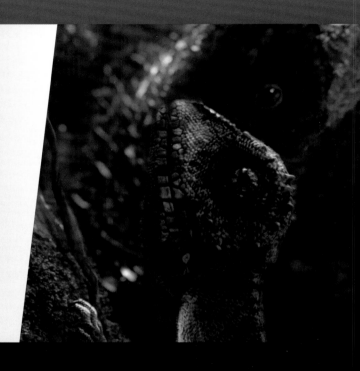

2 In a flurry of activity, the heap of feathers moves, careering down the tree trunk. It is a tree-dwelling dinosaur known as –

▶ *MICRORAPTOR*

and it's hungry.

Its blunt snout snaps at the small lizard, but the *Xianglong* easily avoids capture, scurrying further up the tree.

3 *Microraptor* gives chase, tearing up behind the fleeing lizard, which darts out onto an overhanging branch. Now *Microraptor* has its prey. There's nowhere else for the *Xianglong* to run. Victorious, *Microraptor* clambers up to the branch and time stands still for a second as the two reptiles stare at each other.

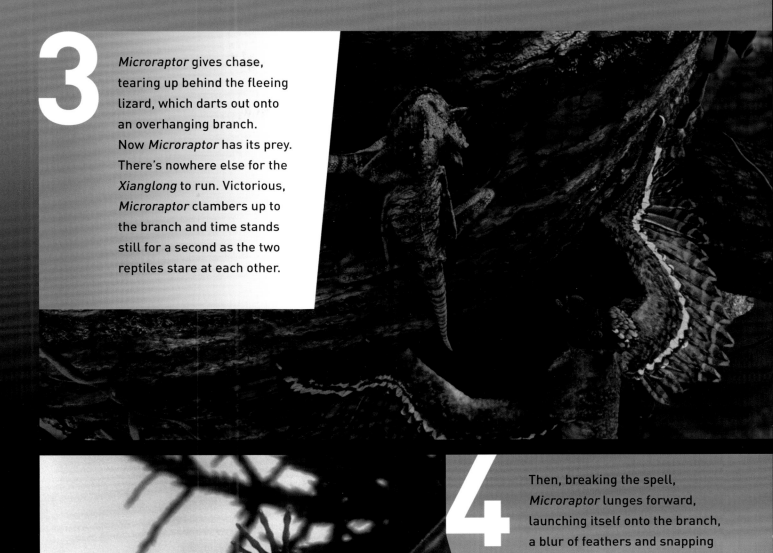

4 Then, breaking the spell, *Microraptor* lunges forward, launching itself onto the branch, a blur of feathers and snapping jaws. But the jaws close on thin air... *Xianglong* has leapt from the branch and is plummeting down towards the forest floor. As *Microraptor* watches its prey tumble downward, a pair of wings flick out from the lizard's ribcage and *Xianglong* glides away to safety.

THE RIB GLIDER

The discovery of *Xianglong* – Chinese for flying lizard - was revealed by Xu Xing and a team of colleagues in early 2007. The remains had been found near Yizhou in China's Liaoning Province, complete with fossilized skin and eight pairs of extraordinarily long dorsal ribs. These bones would have supported its patagia, the membranes of skin that it used to glide from tree to tree. When fully expanded, these wings would have stretched nearly 12 cm (1 foot) across and would have allowed the lizard to glide for distances of up to around 50 metres (164 feet), about half the length of a football pitch.

Whereas most gliding animals, such as flying squirrels, have membranes between their bodies and legs, the use of rib membranes is rare, only found in ancient, lizard-like reptiles from the Late Triassic, between 251 and 199 million years ago, and a large group of gliding lizards that live across modern south-east Asia. *Xianglong*'s patagia seems to share certain shape characteristics with the wings of modern fast-flying birds, suggesting that it was quite agile once it had launched itself into the air. For a tree-dwelling reptile, such a talent was a quick way of getting out of trouble and avoiding would-be predators. But what would *Xianglong* do if the predator could also take to the air? What if the feathers that covered the ravenous *Microraptor* weren't just for show?

5

Microraptor watches *Xianglong* escape. It hesitates for just a second and then leaps off the branch. Falling through the air, *Microraptor* fans out the feathers on its arms and legs to reveal not just one pair of wings, but two. *Microraptor* can also glide.

Unaware it is being followed, *Xianglong* twists its body, banking to the right. *Microraptor* adjusts its legs and arms, perfectly matching *Xianglong*'s flight path. *Xianglong* lands gently on a tree trunk, only metres from the forest floor. Suddenly, it realises that it's in danger. *Microraptor*'s shadow falls over the bark of the tree. Just before *Microraptor* lands, Xianglong shoots up the trunk, running for its life. The chase continues...

PREDATORY GLIDER

CHINA

MICRORAPTOR GUI

TRANSLATION
Gu Zhiwel's small thief

DIET
Carnivore

HABITAT
The woodlands of northern China

ERA
Early Cretaceous, 125–122 million years ago

CLASSIFICATION
Saurischia, Theropoda, Coelurosauria,
Maniraptora, Dromaeosauridae

WEIGHT
1–2 kg (2–4 lb)

LENGTH
80 cm (31 inches)

TAIL

Microraptor probably used its long tail when gliding, moving it up and down to control its descent.

SHOULDERS

Microraptor didn't have powerful flight muscles that would have kept it in the air for long or allowed it to take off from the ground. It needed to glide from high vantage points. *Microraptor* steered itself in the air by moving its limbs. However, it probably wouldn't have been nimble enough to grab prey while in flight.

FAMILY

Microraptor belongs to the theropod family Dromaeosauridae. Dromaeosaurids are sometimes termed 'raptors' but this term is disliked by many experts since the word is already in widespread use for a modern group of animals (the eagles, hawks and falcons).

My-krow-rap-TOR gee

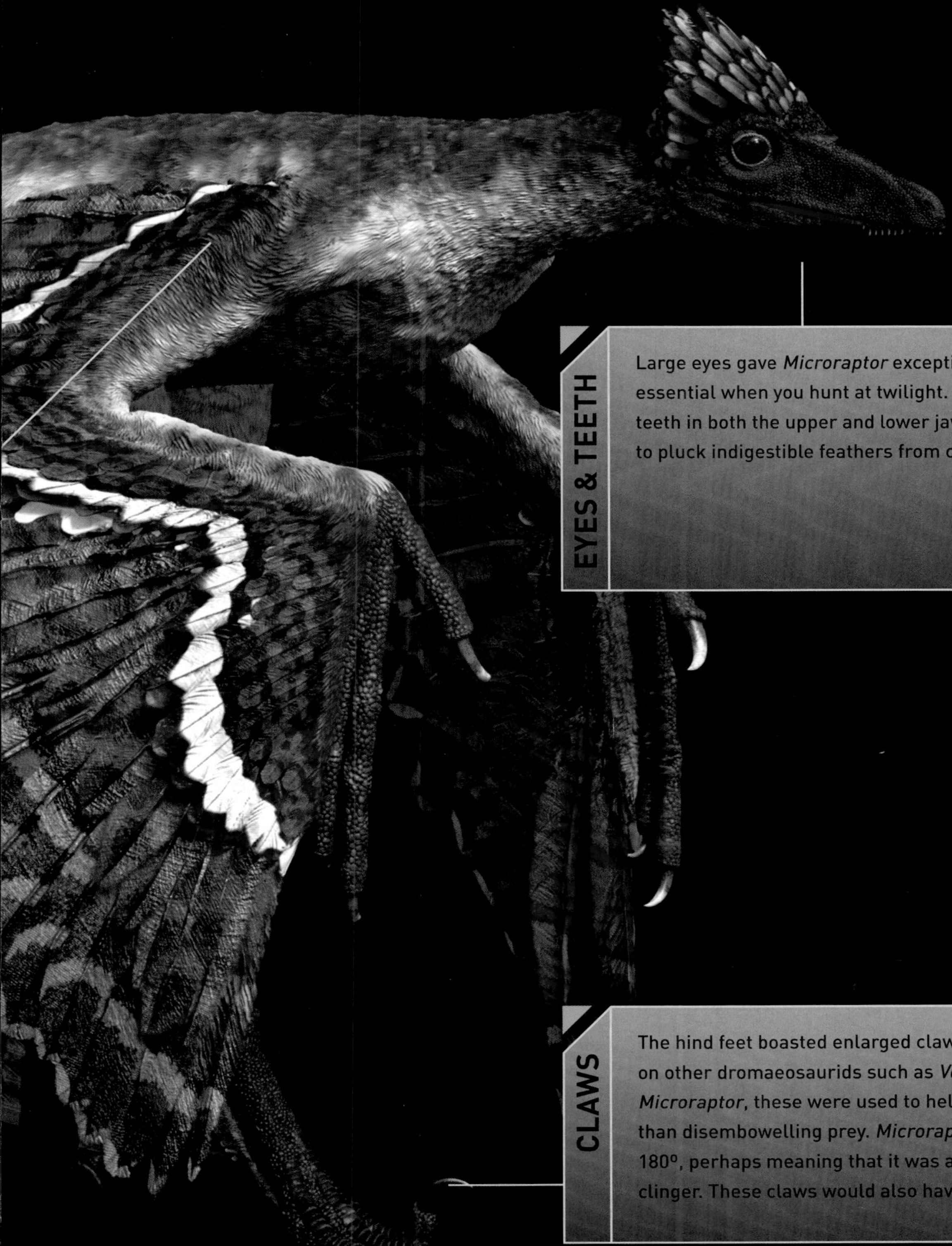

EYES & TEETH

Large eyes gave *Microraptor* exceptionally good vision, essential when you hunt at twilight. Long, curved, serrated teeth in both the upper and lower jaws may have been used to pluck indigestible feathers from corpses.

CLAWS

The hind feet boasted enlarged claws, similar to those found on other dromaeosaurids such as *Velociraptor*. Perhaps, in *Microraptor*, these were used to help tree-climbing rather than disembowelling prey. *Microraptor*'s claws curved around 180°, perhaps meaning that it was a very capable climber and clinger. These claws would also have made short work of prey!

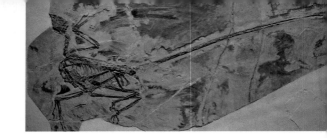

FAMILIAR FEATHERS

When Xu Xing and his colleagues studied the fossils of *Microraptor gui* in 2003 it soon became clear that these feathers weren't there to keep the dinosaur warm or just for show. They were long, vaned and as asymmetrical as the feathers found on modern birds. That wasn't all. These aerodynamic feathers, capable of creating lift in the air, were found on both its arms and legs. Xu and his team realized they were looking at a dinosaur that could glide down from treetops, perhaps covering distances of around 18 metres (60 feet) at a time.

Microraptor gui was a four-winged dinosaur capable of flight.

HOW DID MICRORAPTOR GLIDE?

At first scientists believed that *Microraptor* tucked its legs to its chest and spread out its arms to glide. The pose would have made it looked like a feathered biplane soaring through the forest.

However, recent research from the University of Kansas in the United States and the Northeastern University in China has led to a different idea about this winged wonder. Using a wooden model created from casts of the original *Microraptor* bones, and real-life feathers trimmed to resemble those found in the fossils, the team of scientists created a life-size *Microraptor* model.

The scientists put the model through its paces with the arms and legs held in the biplane position, and also with its hind legs splayed out behind the arms. The model did glide for a short distance when kept in the biplane formation, but it also quickly plummeted to the ground at breakneck speeds.

Yet, with its legs held out behind like a second set of wings, the model made a far gentler and more graceful descent, covering more ground before coming to rest. Some experts therefore think that this is how *Microraptor* flew, with its hind wings stretched out behind the front, working in tandem to keep it in the air. Others argue that it was simply impossible for *Microraptor* to adopt this posture, since the anatomy of its hips and hind leg bones would have prevented the legs from being stretched out sideways in this fashion.

FIRST FLIGHTS

The results of this experiment also added fuel to one of the greatest controversies that exists in the subject of bird evolution. Anatomical evidence demonstrates that birds descended from the carnivorous theropods of the Jurassic period, but how had they first taken to the skies?

HYPOTHESIS ONE: FROM THE GROUND UP

Because theropods have traditionally been imagined as ground-dwelling, fast-running animals, many experts have argued that flight originated on the ground, believing that these swift hunters began to develop the ability to leap higher and higher, flapping their arms to stay in the air. Over millennia they eventually adapted to take flight.

HYPOTHESIS TWO: FROM THE TREES DOWN

Microraptor perhaps shows that birds evolved from tree-climbing theropods that took to leaping from tall branches and gliding. As time passed, early birds developed the powerful muscles they needed to stay in the air rather than just swooping down to the ground.

While *Microraptor* was in its element in the air and could happily scamper up tree trunks and along branches, things were different on the ground. Those feathers on its legs grew to lengths of 17 cm (7 inches) and would presumably have got in the way when walking on the ground. In fact, the forest floor would have been a perilous place for the suddenly cumbersome *Microraptor*. There were other, larger feathered dromaeosaurids on the prowl, predators that had no problem getting around with their feet firmly on the ground – predators such as –

▶ *SINORNITHOSAURUS*

END OF THE LINE

1 After playing cat and mouse in the trees, *Microraptor* finally catches Xianglong. Little does it know that a *Sinornithosaurus* is perched just above. Taking its chance, *Sinornithosaurus* attacks, landing right on top of *Microraptor*.

2 The smaller dinosaur manages to wriggle out of *Sinornithosaurus*'s grip and dives into the air, but it can only glide down to the forest floor.

3 With a crash *Sinornithosaurus* lands behind the fleeing raptor that, held back by its long hind feathers, is struggling to run. *Sinornithosaurus* has no such problem and gives chase. This is a dinosaur that is as happy racing through the undergrowth as it is chasing its prey through the skies.

SINORNITHOSAURUS MILLENII

TRANSLATION
Chinese bird-lizard of the new millennium

DIET
Carnivore

HABITAT
Forests of north-eastern China

ERA
Early Cretaceous, 125–122 million years ago

CLASSIFICATION
Saurischia, Theropoda, Coelurosauria,

Maniraptora, Dromaeosauridae

WEIGHT
3 kg (7 lb)

LENGTH
1.2 metres (4 feet)

FEATHERS

Long, complex feathers covered *Sinornithosaurus*'s long arms and tail, but they weren't used for flight. Perhaps they were used for camouflage or display. Some scientists do think, however, that *Sinornithosaurus* might have also been able to glide for short distances.

DISCOVERY

The discovery of *Sinornithosaurus* was first announced by Xu Xing, Xiao-Ling Wang and Xiao-Chun Wu of the IVPP in 1999. The near-complete skeleton, the first ever recorded of a dromaeosaurid complete with feathers, was found in Liaoning Province, China, in the Yixian Formation.

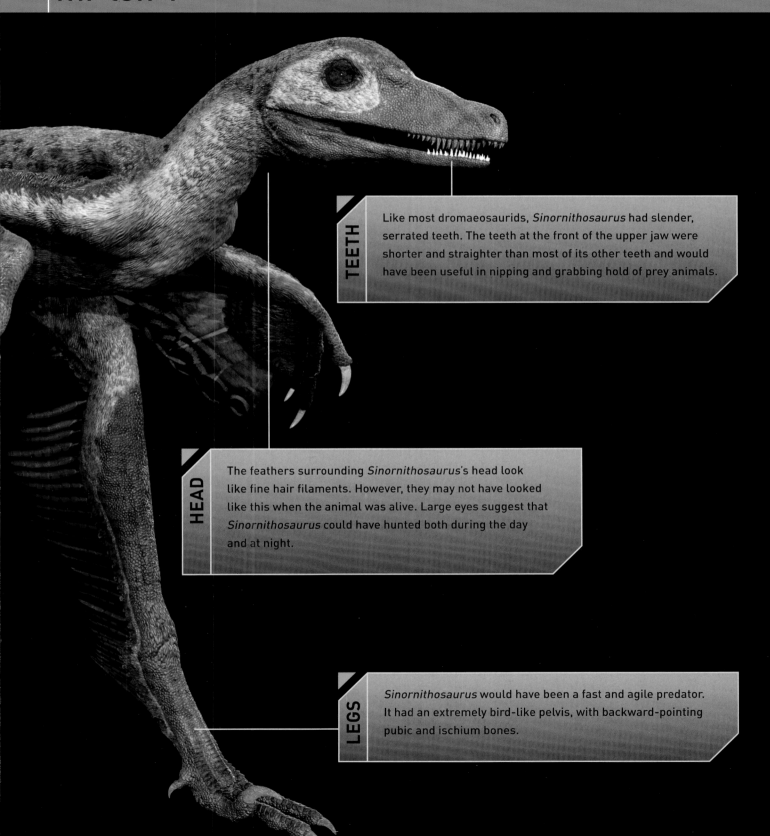

TEETH

Like most dromaeosaurids, *Sinornithosaurus* had slender, serrated teeth. The teeth at the front of the upper jaw were shorter and straighter than most of its other teeth and would have been useful in nipping and grabbing hold of prey animals.

HEAD

The feathers surrounding *Sinornithosaurus*'s head look like fine hair filaments. However, they may not have looked like this when the animal was alive. Large eyes suggest that *Sinornithosaurus* could have hunted both during the day and at night.

LEGS

Sinornithosaurus would have been a fast and agile predator. It had an extremely bird-like pelvis, with backward-pointing pubic and ischium bones.

WHAT COLOURS
WERE THEIR FEATHERS?

The birds of today come in all kinds of different colours, from dull browns and blacks for camouflage to vibrant greens, reds and yellows for display. It's safe to suggest that the plumage of bird-like dinosaurs was the same. But is there any way of finding out just how colourful dinosaurs actually were?

HIDDEN COLOUR

The fossilized feathers found with the remains of *Sinornithosaurus* and *Sinosauropteryx* provided the answer. Fossils don't usually preserve colours, but they do have minuscule evidence locked within their structure.

A team of scientists led by Zhonghe Zhou of Beijing's IVPP and Michael Benton of the University of Bristol, UK, examined the fossilized feathers and found microscopic sacs called melanosomes preserved within the feathers. These are the same tiny objects found in every coloured feather or strand of hair on the planet today, including the hair on your head. The colour of your hair depends on the shape of these melanosomes. If you have sausage-shaped melanosomes, known as eumelanosomes, you're likely to have black or grey hair, but if your hair contains more spherical melanosomes, known as phaeomelanosomes, it will be red or ginger. The same structures, packed with pigments, are also found in birds' feathers.

BEAUTIFUL PLUMAGE

Both types of feathers tested by the scientists were packed with eumelanosomes and phaeomelanosomes. By looking at the concentration of the sacs in both dinosaurs, they worked out that *Sinosauropteryx* would probably have had rusty-orange features, with a series of white stripes on its long tail. *Sinornithosaurus*'s feathers, on the other hand, were a combination of reddish-brown, yellow, black and grey – the perfect colours for hiding in the treetops.

But, this wasn't a dinosaur that hid away for protection. Recent evidence has shown that it may have camouflaged itself to perform the perfect ambush. *Sinornithosaurus* was a predator.

While *Sinornithosaurus* didn't have as many teeth as its close relative, the infamous *Velociraptor*, its bank of sharp fangs were a telltale sign that this was a theropod that enjoyed meat.

But did the teeth of *Sinornithosaurus* do more than just slice through the flesh of its prey? Did they deliver a fatal dose of venom, designed to allow the turkey-sized dino to punch above its weight and bring down much larger prey?

This controversial theory has caused much debate among the scientific community and shows that at times palaeontologists don't always agree about how prehistoric animals ticked.

In 2010, a research team led by Enpu Gong made an extremely interesting proposal about *Sinornithosaurus* and its possible method of killing. They noticed that the fangs near the back of the theropod's upper jaws were especially long and possessed long grooves that, they claimed, were linked to a cavity on the side of the skull. They termed this cavity the 'subfenestral fossa'. The team proposed that this strange combination of features resembled something seen elsewhere – not in dinosaurs, but in modern snakes.

Gong and his colleagues suggested that the teeth recalled those of rear-fanged snakes such as the African tree snake or Boomslang. As you'd expect from the name, the fangs of these snakes are housed at the back of their jaws rather than the front. Front-fanged snakes have hollow fangs that they use to inject venom, whereas the venom of rear-fanged snakes trickles down the outsides of the teeth once the snake has taken a bite.

And we know from the behaviour of living animals that venom doesn't always have to kill. In 2009, Bryan Fry, a venom researcher at the University of Melbourne in Australia, worked together with a team of colleagues to show that Komodo dragons had numerous venom glands in their jaws. It was previously thought that the dragon gave its victims blood poisoning thanks to toxic bacteria believed to thrive inside its mouth. Fry and colleagues actually found that the Komodos possess non-fatal venom that sends their prey into shock, decreasing their blood pressure and leaving them too weak to escape.

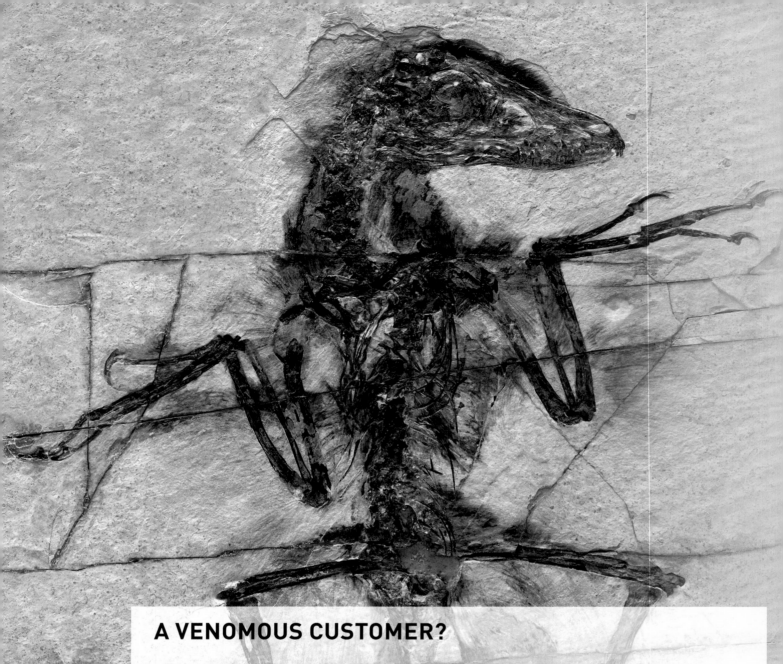

A VENOMOUS CUSTOMER?

Did the small hollow in *Sinornithosaurus*'s skull house a venom gland? Perhaps, the team speculated, the fangs were long enough to pierce through a blanket of feathers to drive half a centimetre (0.2 inches) into the flesh of its prey – deep enough to introduce venom into its bloodstream. And what of the thin groove that, Gong and his colleagues claim, seems to runs the length of the jaw and is supposedly connected to numerous pits located close to the bases of the teeth? Did this help distribute the venom, channelling it to the backward-curving fangs?

Gong's team suggests that the turkey-sized killer lay in wait for its victims on the lower branches of trees, ready to swoop down and plunge its fangs into passing prey. The venom, which was probably not strong enough to kill outright, would seep down the ducts on the teeth into the wound, putting the prey into rapid shock. Immobolized, the terrified animal could do nothing as *Sinornithosaurus* ate it alive. In this way, the feathered predator could bring down prey much larger than itself.

CONFLICTING OPINIONS

While the idea put forward by Gong and his colleagues is unarguably fascinating, it has failed to convince other experts and the pieces of evidence used to support it have not stood up to scrutiny. Several counter-arguments have been put forward to question the three key elements of the argument.

EVIDENCE ONE:
SINORNITHOSAURUS HAD EXTRAORDINARILY LONG REAR FANGS.

Palaeontologists Federico Gianechini, Federico Agnolin and Martin Ezcurra have all argued that *Sinornithosaurus*'s elongated teeth weren't actually especially long. Gong and his colleagues argued that the teeth were made especially long by the fact that the roots partially projected out of the tooth sockets. But in living animals the roots of a tooth never project beyond the gum. It seems that the super-long back teeth of *Sinornithosaurus* were only extraordinarily long because they'd slipped partly out of their sockets. This often happens with theropod fossils.

EVIDENCE TWO:
SINORNITHOSAURUS HAD A VENOM GLAND.

The structure that Gong and his colleagues identified as a 'venom gland' was a damaged, pockmarked area on the side of the face, and concrete evidence for any 'subfenestral fossa' is lacking. Not only is this region of the skull poorly preserved in *Sinornithosaurus*, it seems that various small dromaeosaurids possess similar, pockmarked skull bones.

EVIDENCE THREE:
SINORNITHOSAURUS HAD GROOVES ON ITS FANGS.

Gianechini, Agnolin and Ezcurra argued that the grooves weren't as unique as Gong insists, pointing out similar channels found in other theropods.

In recent years it's become clear that the grooves and channels seen on the teeth of some animals are not necessarily anything to do with venomous behaviour. Modern-day mandrills and baboons, for example, also have grooves on their canines and yet aren't venomous. Instead, these channels make it easier for the primates to plunge their teeth in and out of fruit without causing troublesome suction.

The idea that *Sinornithosaurus* might have delivered a venomous bite was never well supported and the majority of dinosaur experts regarded it as poorly founded right from the start. But however it killed its prey, when *Sinornithosaurus* cornered *Microraptor* on the leaf-strewn forest floor, it's unlikely that the four-winged flyer would have stood much of a chance against its larger, more agile opponent.

CHANGE

Dinosaurs had an extraordinary ability to adapt to, and exploit, any environment. This astonishing capacity to evolve into ever-more diverse and bizarre forms meant that the dinosaurs could spread throughout the world and dominate life upon it completely. It was simply a case of change, or die.

OR DIE

DWARFS
AND GIANTS

Dinosaurs dominated planet Earth for 160 million years, spreading into all four corners of the globe. But what was their secret? What made them such supremely successful animals, able to dominate food chains and hold on to their top position until their near-total extinction 65.5 million years ago?

Part of the answer lies on a Late Cretaceous island in what we now know as Europe. This is Haţeg, an island that eventually became Transylvania. No one really knows how big Haţeg actually was, with estimates ranging between 7,500 and 200,000 sq km (3,000 to 77,000 sq miles), but we do know that it supported a unique and surprising collection of dinosaurs.

Haţeg was an island where nothing was what it first seemed. In 1912, Baron Franz Nopcsa, a Hungarian aristocrat and adventurer, wrote that while the turtles, crocodilians and other small animals of Late Cretaceous Haţeg region grew to normal size, the dinosaurs of the island were stunted, tiny in comparison to their mainland cousins.

A DWARF AMONG GIANTS

Magyarosaurus was a case in point. The first dinosaur bones ever found in Transylvania had been discovered by Nopcsa's sister on their family estate in 1895. Nopcsa studied these bones, naming a number of new species including *Magyarosaurus dacus*. While anatomically similar to the more familiar, gigantic sauropods, Nopcsa theorized that these dinosaurs were dwarfs, no bigger than a horse. Granted, a horse is quite big, but when you compare a horse-sized sauropod to other kinds the difference in size is staggering. At one tonne (1.1 tons), *Magyarosaurus* was one-eighth the mass of close relatives such as the 15 metre (50 feet) long *Ampelosaurus*, and about one-seventieth the mass of its super-sized South American cousin, *Argentinosaurus*.

ARGENTINOSAURUS

For years, many palaeontologists thought that Nopcsa had been wrong: that the skeletons his sister had discovered were just the bones of infant sauropods. However, in 2010 a group of scientists proved that the Baron had been right all along. Professor Mike Benton from the University of Bristol and six other palaeontologists from Romania, Germany and the United States sliced into the bones of a *Magyarosaurus* to study its microstructure. They discovered that the dwarf dinosaurs weren't infants; they were fully grown adults.

THE ISLAND EFFECT

But what led to the Hațeg titanosaur's comparatively tiny size?

Scientists believe it is the very fact that *Magyarosaurus* lived on an island that explains its diminutive size. Animals who find themselves marooned on islands, perhaps by rising sea levels, often shrink over subsequent generations. We've seen it in other lineages of fossil animals, such as the dwarf hippopotamuses and elephants that once lived on the islands of Cyprus, Malta and Sicily in the Mediterranean. Resources are limited, meaning that the animals can either eat themselves into extinction or adapt by becoming smaller and smaller over the generations. The smaller you are, the less food you need.

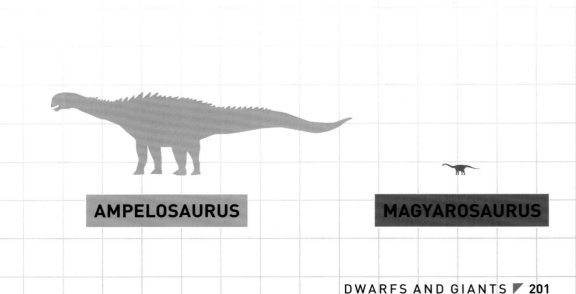

AMPELOSAURUS

MAGYAROSAURUS

DINO SURVIVAL

The dwarf dinosaurs of Hațeg are a fantastic example of the extraordinary ability of dinosaurs to adapt to new environments in order to survive. In doing so they produced some of the weirdest, most alien-looking creatures the world has ever seen.

And the results are often not what you expect. On Hațeg, not all of the native animals shrank in size. Some grew to huge proportions, such as the largest flying vertebrate ever known –

▶ *HATZEGOPTERYX*

HATZEGOPTERYX THAMBEMA

TRANSLATION
Monstrous wing of Hațeg

DIET
Carnivore

HABITAT
Skies of the Hațeg basin, Transylvania

ERA
Late Cretaceous, 70–65 million years ago

CLASSIFICATION
Pterosauria, Pterodactyloidea, Azhdarchidae

WEIGHT
2.4–2.6 tonnes (2.6–2.9 tons)

LENGTH
10–12 metres (33–39 feet)

BODY

As it wasn't restricted to the ground, *Hatzegopteryx* wasn't dwarfed by the island effect. This, along with the lack of large predators, meant that it could grow to gargantuan dimensions. When walking on land, *Hatzegopteryx* would have been similar in height to a giraffe. However, while a giraffe weighs in at around 1 tonne (1 ton), *Hatzegopteryx*'s mass was only around 250 kg (550 lb).

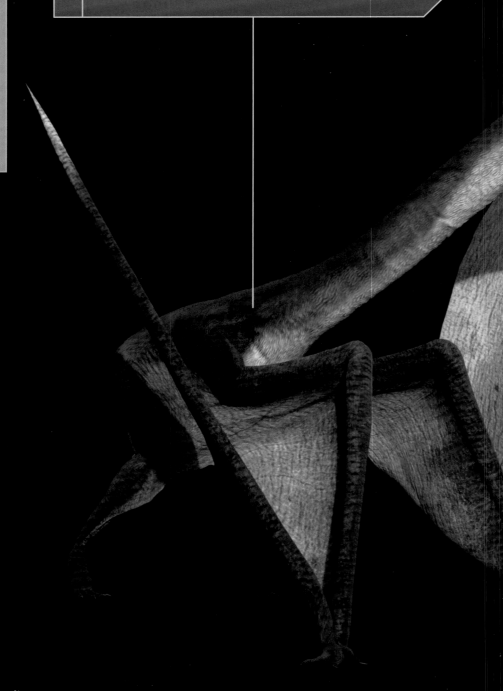

HAT-zeh-GOP-teh-rix
tham-be-ma

SKULL & JAW

The skull of *Hatzegopteryx* was 2–3 metres (6.6–10 feet) long. The skull bones were full of hollows and pits separated by thin, bony struts. Perhaps this lightened the skull and so reduced the amount of energy required to carry it around. The polystyrene-like structure of the skull bones was sturdy but presumably still light enough to allow flight. Its long, narrow jaws could gape incredibly wide.

NECK

Like all of the azhdarchid pterosaurs, *Hatzegopteryx* would have had long, cylindrical neck bones. The result was a very long, slender, rather stiff neck.

SKELETON

Only bits and pieces of *Hatzegopteryx* have been found so far, and nothing like a complete skeleton is known. Parts of the skull, an incomplete left humerus, a femur and various unidentified bone fragments have so far been unearthed. Maybe the reason we've found so few *Hatzegopteryx* bones is that their lightweight structure means they would have rotted away extremely quickly. It's also possible that *Hatzegopteryx* was a rare animal, or one whose remains rarely ended up in places where preservation occurred.

DISCOVERY

Franz Nopcsa reported the discovery of pterosaur remains as early as 1899, but when the skull of the *Hatzegopteryx* was first unearthed during a student dig in Transylvania in the late 1970s, it was mistakenly described as belonging to a theropod. In 2002 a team lead by Dr Eric Buffetaut of the Centre National de la Recherché Scientifique, Paris, France, correctly identified it as that of a huge pterosaur. The name 'thambema' came from the Greek for monster.

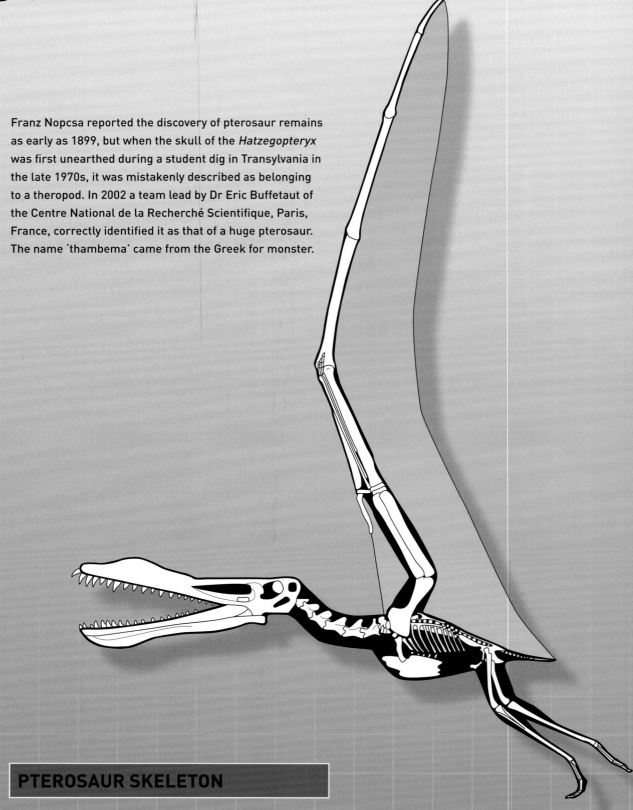

PTEROSAUR SKELETON

EATING ON THE WING?

For years, some scientists believed that pterosaurs, even those as big as *Hatzegopteryx*, fed on the wing, grabbing prey from the water surface while in flight. Recently, however, two arguments have been put forward that challenge this view.

1. Pterosaur skulls lacked the shock-absorbing muscles and extra joints required to protect them from drag as their long jaws hit the water surfaces. It's unlikely that creatures this size would have been able to remain aloft should their jaws have ploughed into the water.

2. In the past it was typically thought that pterosaurs would have been clumsy on the ground. However, in recent years, huge numbers of pterosaur tracks found worldwide have shown that pterosaurs of several kinds were actually highly proficient quadrupedal walkers. (They walked with their wings folded up, with their weight supported on their three-clawed fingers as well as their slim, flat feet.) Tracks found in an abandoned quarry in Hadong County, South Korea, in 2004 and named *Haenamichnus uhangriensis*, have been identified as those of an azhdarchid. The azhdarchid that made the *Haenamichnus* tracks was huge, standing 3 metres (10 feet) at the shoulder with a wingspan of over 10 metres (33 feet). The tracks confirm that pterosaurs like *Hatzegopteryx* were perfectly capable walkers, and they were probably able to run when grounded as well.

The evidence suggests that pterosaurs were as happy on terra firma as they were in the air. These monsters hunted on the ground.

PTEROSAUR
FOOTPRINT

PTEROSAUR
TRACKS

PICKING UP DINNER

1 *Hatzegopteryx* flies high above the Hațeg island, casting a huge shadow on the ground.

2 It soars over the countryside, coming in to land among a herd of tiny magyarosaurs. Walking through the clearing, it spies an infant...

3 ... and plucks the helpless creature from the ground...

4 ... swallowing it whole.

A STRANGE FAMILY

Dinosaurs continued to evolve throughout their long reign, but one weird group was a mystery for decades – the therizinosaurs or 'reaper lizards', named after their long, scythe-like claws. Therizinosaurs have long been a puzzle: they were theropods, closely related to the carnivores *Tyrannosaurus rex* and *Velociraptor*, and yet their peculiar anatomy shows that they were plant eaters, not predators.

A near-complete therizinosaur skeleton uncovered in southern Utah, USA in 2009, helped shed new light on this bizarre and enigmatic family of dinosaurs.

This strange animal was called –

▶ *NOTHRONYCHUS*

NORTH AMERICA

NOTHRONYCHUS GRAFFAMI

TRANSLATION
Graffam's slothful claw

DIET
Herbivore

HABITAT
Utah, USA

ERA
Mid Cretaceous, 92.5 million years ago

CLASSIFICATION
Saurischia, Theropoda, Coelurosauria, Therizinosauridae

WEIGHT
1.2 tonnes (1.3 tons)

LENGTH
5 metres (17 feet)

HEAD & NECK

With long, slender necks, therizinosaurs had small heads with keratinous beaks at their jaw tips filled with tiny, leaf-shaped teeth that had leaf-cutting serrations.

LIMBS

Nothronychus had short, stumpy legs but broad hips to support its giant midriff. It had four-toed feet – the first toe (on the inside of the foot) was unusually large for a theropod.

no-thrown-EYE-kus
GRA-fam-eye

DISCOVERY

The discovery of *Nothronychus graffami* was as curious as the animal's anatomy. Barry Albright of the University of North Florida and David Gillette of the Museum of Northern Arizona were excavating the remains of plesiosaurs and other sea-dwelling animals that once inhabited Utah's Western Interior Seaway 93 million years ago. They had found nothing out of the ordinary until a museum volunteer by the name of Merle Graffam discovered a dinosaur toe bone. When they started to dig, they found the complete skeleton of the *Nothronychus*. It seems somewhat odd that a dinosaur's complete remains came to rest 60 miles from the nearest shoreline, especially when the teeming sea-predators of the region would normally have ripped a floating carcass to shreds. One suggestion is that the dinosaur was carried far out to sea on a huge floating raft of soil and vegetation and eventually drowned when the raft disintegrated.

CLAWS

Massive 22 cm (9 inch) claws could hook around high branches and drag them down. They may have also been used in defence.

BODY

An enormous, barrel-shaped pot belly, housing a massive gut, was ideal for digesting plants and leaves.

TURNING
VEGETARIAN

Why would theropods evolve into plant eaters?

It seems that, once again, adaptation was the key. Therizinosaurs are part of the major theropod group termed Maniraptora, which includes birds, *Velociraptor* and its relatives, and such additional groups as the oviraptorosaurs and scansoriopterygids. It now seems likely that early maniraptorans were omnivorous, devouring both flesh and plant-life.

At some point in their evolution, therizinosaurs such as *Nothronychus* stopped chasing animal prey and began concentrating on the new varieties of plant that were blossoming during Cretaceous times. They became the Cretaceous equivalents of pandas, carving out a niche in a land dominated by ferocious tyrannosaurids. Becoming ever more suited to this new plentiful food source, their legs became stockier and their guts evolved to digest the greenery. The vicious, hooked claws that they retained from their bloodthirsty past, however, now proved useful for stripping foliage from trees, and also came in handy as defensive weapons. Their fat belly and stout legs would have slowed down the therizinosaurs, so new techniques were required for self-defence.

THERIZINOSAUR CLAWS

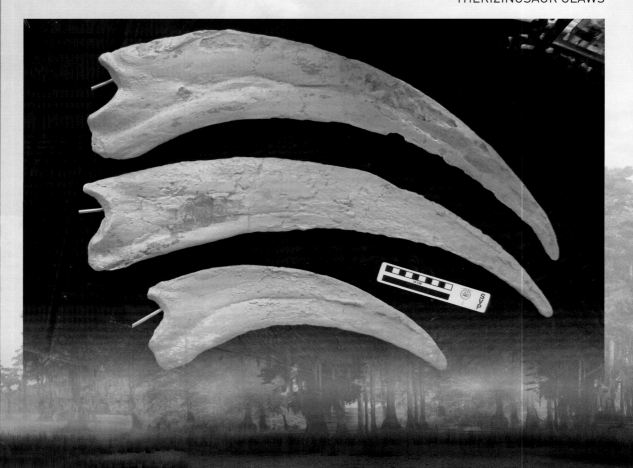

NOTHRONYCHUS EVOLVED OVER TIME UNTIL ITS BODY WAS IDEALLY SUITED TO STRIPPING FOOD FROM THE TREETOPS, WITH ITS HEAVY LEGS AND STOMACH BALANCING ITS LONG NECK, WHICH WOULD HAVE REACHED HIGH INTO THE TREETOPS TO FIND FOOD.

NOTHRONYCHUS

CLAWS OUT FOR BATTLE

1 *Nothronychus* is feasting on the high branches of a tree, taking advantage of the fact that, by standing on two legs, it can reach higher than other herbivores.

But suddenly a hungry tyrannosaurid moves in. The therizinosaur is in grave danger.

2 Facing the predator, *Nothronychus* rears up, lifting its scythe-like claws into the air.

3 The tyrannosaurid charges, but *Nothronychus* is ready. Swiping forward, the therizinosaur rakes its 22 cm (9 inch) claws across the tyrannosaurid's face. Bloodied and wounded, the tyrannosaurid makes its escape.

KING OF
THE CANNIBALS

While therizinosaurs prospered by adapting to a new, herbivorous diet, tyrannosaurids thrived by being the least fussy eaters in history. If they found a dead body, they'd happily take advantage of an unexpected feast. It's always easier not to have to kill.

But was the King of the Tyrant Lizards partial to a spot of cannibalism? In 2010, Dr Nick Longrich of Yale University was examining *Tyrannosaurus rex* bones when he discovered massive gouges, clearly made by the teeth of an enormous predator. And only one predator had teeth the right size for these scars – *T. rex* itself. These were the marks of cannibalism.

We have no way of knowing if the two tyrannosaurids fought to the death. The hungry hunter may have just stumbled upon a *T. rex* corpse and fancied a snack. Either way, the evidence is damning. *Tyrannosaurus rex* wasn't beneath feeding on its own flesh and blood.

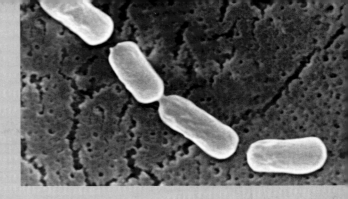

CLOSTRIDIUM
BOTULINUM

INVISIBLE ASSASSIN

However, a bone bed located along Badger Creek in Glacier County, Montana, showed that indiscriminate feeding can have dramatic consequences. Scavenging can sometimes hold hidden dangers. When finding a fresh corpse, a dinosaur would have no idea of what had finished off its serendipitous meal in the first place. What if there was an invisible killer at work?

The site – known as Jack's Birthday Site – yielded over 1,600 identifiable vertebrates. Fossil crocodilians, turtles and fish were all found, but the majority of the bones belonged to dinosaurs, specifically carnivorous troodons and tyrannosaurids. 74 million years ago, the bone bed would have been a stagnant lake and a potential death trap to predators attracted by the lure of an easy meal.

In the modern world, birds sometimes die in their hundreds or thousands following infection from fast-acting and deadly bacteria. The resulting illness is known as botulism. The bacteria grow inside carcasses and are then passed on to maggots. These are then eaten by the birds. When their own infected bodies become riddled with maggots, the deadly cycle begins again.

TOXIC FEAST

It might be that this is what caused the massive accumulation of Cretaceous fossils at Jack's Birthday Site. The bacteria multiplied within the body of a dinosaur that had drowned in the water. Scavengers such as tyrannosaurids then fed on the infected carcass. The bacteria were passed on with swift and fatal effect and, as the infected bodies piled up, more and more predators moved in. Animals that feed on plant life – like *Nothronychus* – were relatively safe from the microscopic assassin, unless they took a sip of the bacterium-laden water.

TOP OF THE FOOD CHAIN

Theropods, the two-legged, bird-like dinosaurs and birds, were the most diverse of all the dinosaur groups. All the familiar predators were part of this great group, as were the peculiar therizinosaurs, the small, tree-living dromaeosaurids, and the bird-like oviraptorosaurs. Over the millennia, theropods evolved into an incredible variety of shapes and sizes.

During the later part of the Cretaceous, tyrannosaurids became the dominant theropod predators, eventually taking the roles previously occupied by carcharodontosaurians, spinosaurids and other giant theropods. It seems that tyrannosaurids got a lucky break, and quickly evolved into ferocious giants. Recent research by Greg Erickson has provided huge advances in our understanding of tyrannosaurid biology. It seems that monsters like *Daspletosaurus*, *Gorgosaurus*, *Albertosaurus* and *Tyrannosaurus* lived surprisingly fast-paced lives.

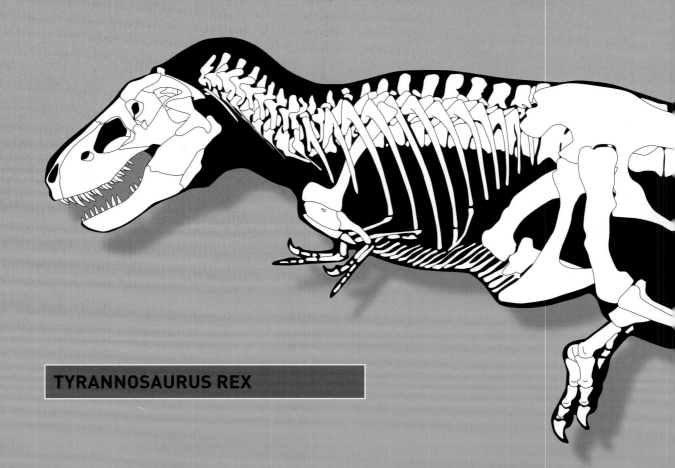

TYRANNOSAURUS REX

A LIFE OF TYRANNY

0–2 years – At this young age, tyrannosaurids were at their most vulnerable, only reaching between 5 and 10 per cent of their final size. However, by the time they reached two years of age, they would already have outgrown the phase when they were most vulnerable to predators.

2–15 years – Tyrannosaurids entered their teenage years. By 15, they would have reached sexual maturity and gained about 80 per cent of their final body mass. Even as a teenager, a tyrannosaurid could easily have matched most mid-size predators. Teenage tyrannosaurids were quicker and more agile than fully grown adults.

16–30 years – After a rapid growth spurt where they put on over two kilos (4.4 lb) a day, tyrannosaurids would have achieved full body size. Little growth occurred after this point, as most energy would have been expended on mating, but what adult tyrannosaurids lacked in agility they would have made up for in sheer, brute force. By this point, they were the undisputed apex predators of their habitat and well able to dominate or out-compete the other predators of the time.

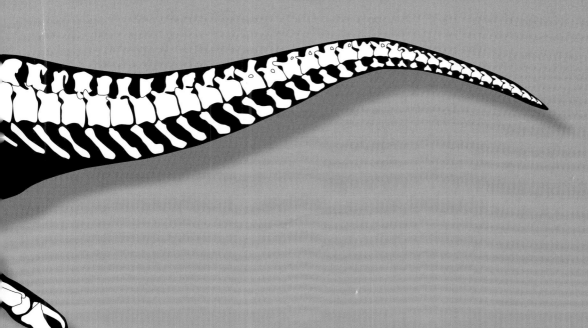

A BROODING PARENT

Other than tyrannosaurids, giant predatory theropods were mostly absent from the Late Cretaceous world. However, small theropods and large omnivorous or herbivorous species flourished. Among the most successful were the oviraptorosaurs, a large number of which inhabited what is now Mongolia. As omnivores – eating both plants and animals – they didn't compete with tyrannosaurids for food. Some, like *Gigantoraptor*, were so successful that they grew to huge proportions.

We don't know much about the biology or behaviour of this group of feathered dinosaurs, but one thing we do know is that they built nests.

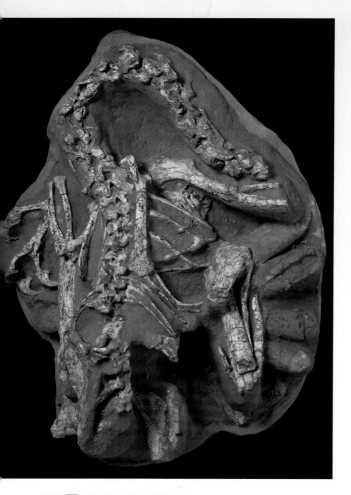

BIG MAMA

In the mid 1990s a series of joint expeditions to the Ukhaa Tolgod region of south-western Mongolia by the American Museum of Natural History and the Mongolian Academy of Sciences unearthed a number of oviraptorosaur skeletons. One of the best of these was nicknamed 'Big Mama' by the palaeontologists. The three metre (10 foot) long dinosaur, later identified as belonging to the species *Citipati osmolskae*, was sat on top of a clutch of 22 long eggs arranged in pairs around the circular nest. The *Citipati*'s legs were folded beneath its body and its arms were spread out, seemingly in a protective posture around its eggs. The pose was exactly the same as that found in modern birds. This dinosaur was brooding.

BIG MAMA

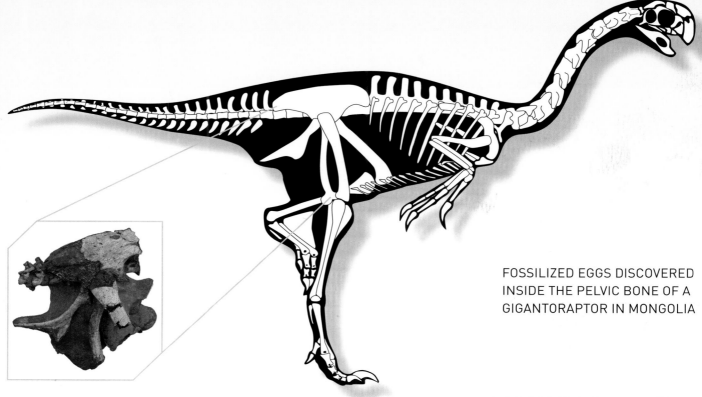

WHY BROOD?

By taking care of its eggs, this dinosaur was surely giving its young a helping hand when it came to survival. Animals such as Gigantoraptor produced massive eggs, over 45 cm (18 inches) long, and the larger the egg, the more developed the hatchling would eventually be, making it far less susceptible to predation.

The snag is that larger eggs take longer to hatch – perhaps as long as 80 days for a creature like *Gigantoraptor*. This long incubation period is consistent with the idea that the parent stayed to guard the eggs and protect them against predators.

Is this the reason why the remains of dinosaurs found brooding eggs show a complete absence of medullary tissue – the bone tissue used to produce eggshell? All the brooding dinos found so far have been identified as males. Apparently, Big Mama was more likely Big Daddy...

FOSSILIZED EGGS DISCOVERED INSIDE THE PELVIC BONE OF A GIGANTORAPTOR IN MONGOLIA

ULTIMATE DEFENCE

1 A brooding *Gigantoraptor* shelters his eggs, the long feathers on his arms keeping them warm at night and cool in the day.

2 Suddenly he senses danger. Two alectrosaurs – the dominant tyrannosaurid in the region – are approaching. The oviraptosaur flattens himself against the ground, trying to hide.

3 When that doesn't work, he goes on the offensive, flapping his great wings to frighten off the predators.

4 One of the alectrosaurs manages to grab the *Gigantoraptor* by the leg, but is dispatched by a hefty kick. Realizing that the *Gigantoraptor* isn't going to submit any time soon, the alectrosaurs retreat to find an easier target.

BURIED
ALIVE

Sometimes danger for a brooding parent doesn't come from a predator. Disaster can strike from the most unlikely places.

In Mongolia, Big Mama was killed not by a hunter, but by the weather. Scientists believe that the dinosaur met its end in the middle of a sudden downpour. Big Mama stretched out its arms to try and shield its eggs from the torrential rain, only to be buried as a mass of water-drenched sand slid down from a nearby dune, entombing parent, nest and eggs together.

While it might seem tragic that dinosaurs were buried alive while protecting their young, such events provide us with the best evidence we have that the habit of brooding eggs evolved not within birds, but deep within theropod history. It's a breeding strategy that's so successful that modern birds still use it today.

BORN
SURVIVORS

The dinosaur discoveries of recent years have revealed these spectacular animals' astonishing capacity for survival. They endured the breakup of continents, outlived extreme climate changes and flourished against all odds, unchecked by rising sea levels and environmental shifts. They dominated life on planet dinosaur for 160 million years and can be considered the most successful animals ever to evolve. Indeed, thanks to their survival to the present as birds, they remain one of the most successful groups of animals alive today.

And yet, despite their miraculous adaptability, the vast majority of the dinosaur groups were ultimately doomed...

DEATH FROM
THE STARS

65.5 million years ago land-living dinosaurs were wiped out by a cataclysmic event, only birds surviving. The reason for the sudden disappearance of most dinosaur groups has been the subject of fierce debate for decades. Was increased volcanic activity to blame? Did toxic algae poison the Earth's oceans? Or did the planet's climate change so drastically that it could no longer support life?

In 2010, a panel of 41 international experts reviewed over 20 years of research and declared once and for all that the dinosaurs were wiped out by a massive asteroid striking the planet and literally creating hell on Earth.

The devastating power of the impact is almost too great to imagine.

Travelling at 19 km (12 miles) per second – 20 times faster than a speeding bullet – the 14 km (9 mile) wide asteroid smashed into Earth at a location called Chicxulub on the Yucatan Peninsula, Mexico. The impact released the same amount of energy as 100 trillion tonnes (110 trillion tons) of TNT, the equivalent of more than a billion atomic weapons. The crater it left is 180 km (112 miles) in diameter and is surrounded by circular fault lines around 240 km (150 miles) in diameter.

THE AFTER EFFECT

Any creature near Yucatan would have been instantly roasted in the blast, but the ongoing effects were just as disastrous. Wild fires raged across Earth's continents, while earthquakes measuring more than 10 on the Richter scale turned the land upside down and created huge tsunamis out at sea. Worst of all, the toxic material thrown up by the impact choked the entire planet, plunging Earth into a global winter that lasted for four months.

NEVER-ENDING WINTER

Shrouded in ash, Earth was cut off from sunlight. All plant life would have withered and died within weeks. The massive herbivores were the first to suffer, with the fast-growing sauropods, the duck-billed hadrosaurs, horned ceratopsians and others soon starving to death. Scavengers fared better, feasting on a glut of dead flesh, but after a while, even this surplus would have become exhausted. As the food ran out, the entire food chain collapsed. Virtually all life on Earth was affected, with over 75 per cent of all species wiped out.

But it was the dinosaurs' sheer size that sealed their fate. Hardly any land animal heavier than 25 kg (55 lb) survived the effects of the impact. Dinosaurs had colonized every corner of the planet, adapting, surviving, thriving. If the asteroid hadn't hit, there's every chance that they would have continued to evolve into even more bizarre and thrilling creatures over time, but we will never know. A freak accident, an unexpected, unprecedented extra-terrestrial event, finally brought about the end of Planet Dinosaur.

But history shows us that life always fights back. With the land-living dinosaurs gone, the mammals that had lived in their shadows inherited the Earth, living alongside the avian dinosaurs that soon took to the skies. They exploded in size and number, spreading out across the surface of the world.

A new age of monsters was just beginning...

THE DINOSAURS
IN CONTEXT

First vertebrates and fish

First land plants and land animals

First sharks and amphibians

First reptiles and insects

Large reptiles

CAMBRIAN (543–490)	ORDOVICIAN (490–443)	SILURIAN (443–417)	DEVONIAN (417–354)	CARBONIFEROUS (354–290)	PERMIAN (290–248)

PALAEOZOIC
'Ancient Life'

At the start of the Palaeozoic era, 543 million years ago, animals began to form hard parts such as shells in their bodies. Throughout the era, plant life developed and fish flourished. The first reptiles and insects evolved and by the Permian epoch, large reptiles roamed Earth. The Palaeozoic era ended with the largest extinction event in history, giving way to the Mesozoic era – the Age of Dinosaurs. The Earth at this time was exceptionally warm and this helped to create the perfect environment for the evolution and diversification of animal species.

MESOZOIC
'Middle Life' or 'The Age of Dinosaurs'

JURASSIC (205–142)

- Early
- Middle — Epidexipteryx (168–152)
- Late — Stegosaurus (156–140), Allosaurus (155–145), Kimmerosaurus (147), Predator X (147), Camptosaurus (147), Diplodocus (155–145)

First mammals
First birds

CRETACEOUS (142–65)

- Early — Microraptor (125–122), Sinornithosaurus (125–122), Sarcosuchus (110), Ouranosaurus (110), Iguanodon (144–112)
- Late — Mapusaurus (99), Spinosaurus (99–93), Carcharodontosaurus (98–93), Paralititan (98), Nothronychus (95–92), Argentinosaurus (95), Gigantoraptor (80), Daspletosaurus (76–72), Chasmosaurus (76–70), Oviraptor (75), Edmontosaurus (71–65), Troodon (71–65), Majungasaurus (70), Hatzegopteryx (70–65), Velociraptor (80–70), Tyrannosaurus rex (67–65)

First snakes

By the end of this period, the basis of modern life was
in place. The end of the Mesozoic era saw another mass
extinction that wiped most dinosaurs from the face of
the Earth, leaving only birds as survivors. But in the new
Cenozoic era, modern animals evolved to take the place of
the once-dominant dinosurs. This was the age of humans.

First modern mammals
First hominid fossils

Neanderthal and
Cro-Magnon man

TERTIARY
(65–1.8)

QUARTERNARY
(1.8–0.01)

CENOZOIC
'New Life'

THE MODERN
WORLD VIEW

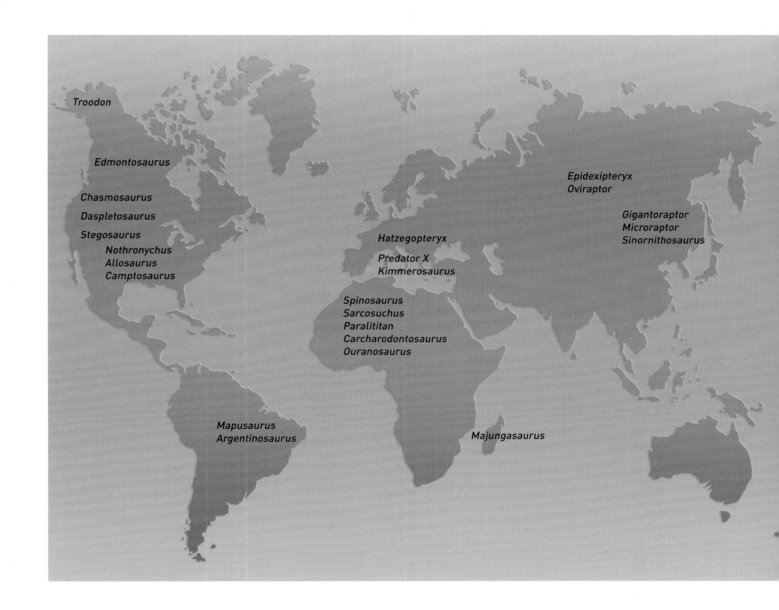

Troodon

Edmontosaurus

Chasmosaurus

Daspletosaurus

Stegosaurus
Nothronychus
Allosaurus
Camptosaurus

Epidexipteryx
Oviraptor

Gigantoraptor
Microraptor
Sinornithosaurus

Hatzegopteryx

Predator X
Kimmerosaurus

Spinosaurus
Sarcosuchus
Paralititan
Carcharodontosaurus
Ouranosaurus

Mapusaurus
Argentinosaurus

Majungasaurus

INDEX

This book is published to accompany the television series entitled *Planet Dinosaur*, first broadcast on BBC1 in 2011

Executive Producer: Andrew Cohen
Series Producer: Nigel Paterson
Assistant Producer: Catherine Wyler
Production Manager: Beth Ambrose

All digital images and landscape art created by Jellyfish Pictures Ltd
www.jellyfishpictures.co.uk for BBC Worldwide Ltd

10 9 8 7 6 5 4 3 2 1

Published in 2011 by BBC Books, an imprint of Ebury Publishing.
A Random House Group Company

The Random House Group Limited Reg. No. 954009

Addresses for companies within the Random House Group can be found at www.randomhouse.co.uk

A CIP catalogue record for this book is available from the British Library.

ISBN 978 1 84 990093 5

The Random House Group Limited supports the Forest Stewardship Council® (FSC®), the leading international forest certification organisation. All our titles that are printed on Greenpeace approved FSC® certified paper carry the FSC® logo. Our paper procurement policy can be found at www.randomhouse.co.uk/environment

Commissioning editor: Muna Reyal
Project editor: Caroline McArthur
Specialist reader: Dr Darren Naish
Designer: Aaron Blecha
Digital images: Jellyfish Pictures Ltd
Production: David Brimble

Colour origination by: Dot Gradations
Printed and bound in Germany by Firmengruppe APPL, Wemding, Germany

To buy books by your favourite authors and register for offers, visit www.randomhouse.co.uk

All digital images produced by Jellyfish Pictures Ltd for the BBC. All landscape art created by Chris Rosewarne (Jellyfish Pictures Ltd.)

All dinosaur models © Jellyfish Pictures Ltd. 13 t & b © Natural History Museum; 23 © Kristian Remes et al.; 33 created from source material © Paul Sereno; 34–35 created from source material © Karen Carr; 35 r © www.projectexploration.org; 58 © Louie Psihoyos; 54 r © Nizar Ibrahim, University College Dublin; 59 created from source material © Royal Tyrrell, Museum, Drumheller, Canada; 60–61 © Paul Sereno; 61 m Nizar Ibrahim, University College Dublin; 70–71 © Russell Hawley; 91 © Lukas Panzarin; 95 © Corbin17/Alamy; 99 © Cyril Ruoso/JH Editorial; 104–105 created from source material © Patrick O'Connor; 114 © The Natural History Museum, London; 126–7 t & b created from source material by Adam Smith Plesiosauria.com; 129 l © Louie Psihoyos; 129 r © Jörn Geister; 130 © Gabbro/Alamy; 138 © James E. Martin, South Dakota School of Mines and Technology; 144–5 © Louie Psihoyos; 145 b © Louie Psihoyos; 148 © Louie Psihoyos; 155 t & b created from source material by Jon Stone; 164 © Vova Pomortzeff/Alamy; 168 Fucheng Zhang; 176 © AFP/Getty Images; 188 © Corbin17/Alamy; 189 © David A. Burnham; 194 University of Bristol; 196 © Mick Ellison; 197 © National Geographic Image Collection/Alamy; 207 t & b © Koo Guen Hwang; 212 © Jim Kirkland; 214 © Lindsay Zanno; 215 © Lindsay Zanno; 219 t © BSIP SA/Alamy; 220–221 based on source material © Greg Paul; 222 © Mick Ellison; 223 t © Ken Carpenter; 223 b © AP/Press Association.

The author and publisher gratefully acknowledge the permission granted to reproduce the copyright material in this book. Every effort has been made to trace copyright holders and to obtain their permission for the use of copyright material. The publisher apologizes for any errors or omissions in the above list and would be grateful if notified of any corrections that should be incorporated in future reprints or editions of this book.

SPECIAL THANKS

Thanks to my editors, Dino-Queens Caroline McArthur and Muna Reyal.

Also *Spinosaurus*-sized shout-outs to Sally Palmer (for being an unofficial scientific advisor) and Peter Travers, George Mann and Mark Wright (for being officially good chaps and brilliant support).

And finally, as always, big hugs to the three dinosaur-loving ladies of my life: Clare, Chloe and Connie. Watch out for the naughty dinosaurs, girls!

BBC Books would like to thank Andrew Cohen, Beth Ambrose and Catherine Wyler at the BBC; Mark Sherwood, Phil Dobree and the team at Jellyfish Pictures; Cav Scott; Aaron Blecha; Darren Naish and Steve Tribe.